AMERICA'S OUTLAWS

and the Treasures They Left Behind

by

W. C. Jameson

illustrations by
Shelby Marie Vaughn

August Hou
ATLAN

Introduction

Americans have long been fascinated with outlaws. Many Americans can't tell you who their congressman is or who the fortieth president was, but they can name any number of prominent outlaws and recite their deeds. Who does not know of Billy the Kid, Jesse James, Butch Cassidy, the Dalton Gang, and others? The exploits and tales, the lives and times, of these colorful characters have been memorialized in thousands of books, articles, and films. We love our outlaws; we are attracted to their daring and adventurous escapades; we cheer them on as they break the rules and escape from their pursuers. We read books and watch movies about them. Of all of the historical characters associated with America, outlaws remain at or near the top of the list, as far as generating interest among Americans. We can't seem to get enough of them.

In addition to outlaws, another fascination held by Americans is related to lost and buried treasure. This attraction is exploding with the recent proliferation of books, articles, television shows, documentaries, and films on this subject. Combine the allure and mystery of lost and buried treasures with America's outlaws and the result is a collection of tales and accounts featuring compelling and adventurous characters and their incredible fortunes, many of which they had to leave behind. People are still searching for these lost treasures today.

Featured in the following pages are more than two dozen outlaws, accounts of one or more of their daring robberies, and the subsequent caching or loss of a fortune in gold or silver coins or ingots. Due to a variety of circumstances, these outlaws were never able to return to their caches and retrieve the booty. The accounts that follow tell of lost and buried treasures associated with outlaws Frank and Jesse James, the Dalton Gang, the Doolin Gang, Black Jack Ketchum, Sam Bass, Belle Starr, John J. Glanton, Tiburcio Vasquez, the pirate Jean Lafitte, the Apache Indian Victorio, Henry Plummer, Curly Bill Brocius, Ella Watson, and more.

Chapter 1

The Buried Treasure of
the Dalton Gang

One of the most successful outlaw bands in the history of the United States was the Dalton Gang. It was comprised of brothers Bob, Grat, and Emmett, along with an oft-changing cast of two to three additional members. Bob, Grat, and Emmett started out as lawmen, but one day in 1890 when they went to collect their paychecks and found they were not forthcoming, they quit and decided to become outlaws.

Known primarily as a train robber, their leader, Bob Dalton, decided to expand the gang's horizons. An ambitious outlaw, Bob, who wanted to be as famous as Jesse James, decided to attempt a crime unlike anything James had ever accomplished; Bob decided to rob two banks back-to-back in one town in broad daylight. He set his sights on the C. M. Condon & Company Bank and the First National Bank, both in Coffeeville, Kansas.

Within minutes, at least a dozen armed lawmen, along with citizens, were watching the two banks from shop windows, rooftops, and shaded alleys.

Fifteen minutes after the Dalton Gang entered the banks, they had filled several sacks with coins and currency and readied themselves for a dash toward their tethered horses. An employee of one of the banks delayed the robbers by convincing them that the safe was on a time lock and could not be opened for another 45 minutes. During the delay, additional townspeople were recruited.

As the gang members exited through the wide front door of each bank, they were surprised by the sudden barrage of gunfire as the lawmen and citizens opened up on them. With bullets kicking up dust all around them and slamming into the fronts of the banks, the outlaws hesitated only a moment before attempting to sprint toward their horses. A second later, Grat Dalton was gunned down by a shot from Marshal Connelly. As Grat fell, he returned fire, his bullet striking the lawman in the chest and killing him.

Within seconds, the armed crowd grew in excess of 100. Into their midst ran Bill Power, carrying several sacks of coins and trying to reach his horse. The crowd was so dense that Power had to fight his way through the throng. It was only a matter of seconds before he was shot down, dead as he hit the ground, coins spilling out of the sacks. Power had been struck by more than a dozen bullets.

Two Coffeeville residents – Lucas Baldwin and George Cubine – saw Marshal Connelly go down and ran to his aid. Both men were shot and killed by Dick Broadwell. In the process, Broadwell was shot several times but managed to make it across the street to his horse. As he climbed onto his mount, he dropped the sack of money he was carrying.

Though badly wounded, Broadwell spurred his horse and raced out of town. Several Coffeeville residents mounted up and went after him.

From the window of the First National Bank, Bob and Emmett Dalton watched the carnage for a few seconds, then turned and dashed out the back door of the building. At the same time, a group of armed men led by Charles Brown was running up the alley toward the same door. Spotting the on-coming townsmen, Bob Dalton raised his revolver and shot Brown in the forehead, killing him instantly. The men follow-ing Brown did not hesitate, and opened fire, the impact of the bullets knocking Bob to the ground and severely wound-ing Emmett.

As unlikely as it seems, Emmett Dalton, with over a dozen bullet wounds, fought his way through the group of armed men, around the building, across the street, and to his horse. After climbing into the saddle, he raced back toward the alley in an attempt to rescue his brother, receiving several more bullet wounds along the way. After reaching Bob, he at-tempted to pull him up on the horse and behind the saddle. Weakened from his wounds, Bob tried to scramble onto the horse when he was shot in the back. As he died, he fell from the horse, landing heavily on the ground. Hemmed in the alley by men approaching from both ends, Emmett was shot several more times before falling from his horse.

While Emmett was trying to rescue Bob, Dick Broadwell, gushing blood from a dozen wounds, managed to ride a mile out of town before he fell from his saddle. By the time his half-dozen pursuers reached him a moment later, he was dead.

Back in town, the gunfire ceased and the pall of gun smoke began clearing, aided by a soft breeze. Cautious townsfolk approached the fallen bandits, handguns and rifles at the ready. All were dead except for Emmett Dalton, who lay unconscious. In spite of suffering 27 wounds from rifle and revolver bullets as well as shotgun blasts, he survived.

The following day, Bob and Grat Dalton, along with Dick Broadwell and Bob Power, were buried in Coffeeville's Elmwood Cemetery. Before being interred, their corpses were placed side-by-side on a wooden walkway and photographed. As the interment took place, Emmett Dalton was regaining consciousness on a cot in the office of the town's physician. His wounds were treated and he recovered sufficiently to face trial for his role in the attempted robberies and the killings. He was convicted and sentenced to life in prison at the Kansas State Penitentiary in Lansing.

Emmett Dalton, one of the most famous train and bank robbers in the history of the United States, turned out to be a model prisoner. As a result of his good behavior, he was released in 1907 after serving 15 years. Following his release, a number of lawmen followed Dalton for several months in the belief that he would lead them to the location where he had buried the gold and silver coins before attempting the Coffeeville bank robberies. As far as is known, Dalton never returned to the Onion Creek site.

Dalton moved to Tulsa, where he worked for a short time as a security guard. Later, he opened a butcher shop. Not long afterward, he moved to California where he sold real estate, wrote a book, and obtained small parts in a handful of western movies.

The exact location of the Onion Creek treasure site has been disputed over the years, but recently discovered information has narrowed the search. On the day before they rode into Coffeeville, the Dalton Gang was seen passing through the P. L. Davis ranch, located near the state boundary just outside the town of South Coffeeville. After riding past the Davis residence, they proceeded across a freshly plowed field and into a dense thicket of trees on the west bank of Onion Creek. After getting a small fire started to make coffee, two of the outlaws rode to the nearby farm of J. F. Savage to purchase some grain for their horses.

Just after dawn the following day, Mary Brown, the young daughter of another nearby rancher, was out on a morning ride with a brand-new horse when she heard voices coming from somewhere near Onion Creek. Pulling her mount to a stop, she listened intently and overheard the sounds of men eating breakfast and saddling their mounts. A few minutes later, according to Mary, five horsemen came riding out from under the small wooden bridge that spanned the creek. As she sat on her horse behind the cover of some trees, Mary watched the strangers gallop toward Coffeeville.

Years later, when Mary Brown was an adult, she heard the story of the $20,000 in gold and silver coins being buried near the Dalton Gang's campsite at Onion Creek. She realized the site had been near the bridge and believed she could find it. During the time that had passed since the Coffeeville robbery attempt, however, the old wooden bridge had been torn down, the road relocated, and portions of the creek had changed course. Though she searched throughout the area for a full day, she was unable to identify the place where she had observed the Dalton Gang so many years earlier.

The gold and silver coins buried at the Onion Creek location over a century and a quarter ago most likely still lie in the ground where they were placed by the Daltons. To this day, the treasure lures hopeful seekers, but thus far remains hidden.

Chapter 2

Bill Doolin's Lost Gold Coin Cache

The members of the Doolin Gang were occasional cohorts of the Daltons, and the two groups of outlaws sometimes exchanged members. Bill Doolin, the acknowledged leader of the gang, was once an effective member of the Dalton Gang. For a time, the Doolin Gang was regarded as a collection of the most efficient and notorious outlaws to ever terrorize banks, railroads, and stagecoaches throughout Kansas, Oklahoma, Missouri, and Texas.

Unlike many outlaws of the day, Bill Doolin never spent his loot on women, liquor, or gambling. Instead, this legendary bandit was a devoted family man and extremely frugal with his money. According to some accounts, Bill Doolin was a miser. In spite of having netted more than $175,000 in robberies over the two-year period preceding his death, Doolin lived sparely and apparently buried the bulk of his fortune near a frame shack located in Burden, Kansas. Because Doolin was killed before he was able to retrieve this money, all in gold coins, it likely still lies there today.

During one extended spree of robberies, the Doolin Gang netted $11,000 from a bank in Spearville, Kansas. Two days later they arrived in Cimarron, where they robbed $14,000 from that town's bank. Doolin then led his band to Southwest City, Missouri, and took $15,000 from that bank. On the way to one of their hideouts in Oklahoma, the gang passed through the town of Pawnee, where they robbed the city bank of several more thousands of dollars in gold coins. Following this series of robberies, the bandits rode to Longview, Texas, where they took over $50,000 from another bank.

When they were not robbing banks, the Doolin Gang turned their attention to stagecoaches and trains. Using dynamite to blast open express cars, they held up three trains near Wharton, Oklahoma, and a railroad depot at Woodward.

Bill Doolin was admired and respected by his gang members, but he developed a reputation of being very stingy when it came time to divide the loot. He doled out relatively small portions to his men and kept the largest percentage for himself. While the other gang members visited towns and spent freely on women and alcohol, Doolin remained in camp counting his money.

During a series of train robberies in Kansas, Doolin encountered the small and somewhat isolated community of Burden in Cowley County, 40 miles southeast of Wichita. There, he purchased a plot of land on which stood a weathered frame house. When Doolin was not roaming the countryside robbing banks and trains, he retreated to this quiet place and lived in peace and seclusion. By all accounts, it was near this shack that Doolin buried the greatest portion of his stolen loot.

In December 1895, Doolin traveled to Eureka Springs, Arkansas, a thriving resort town. There he intended to relax in the spring waters, following his series of successful robberies. Though still a relatively young man, Doolin suffered from arthritis and often journeyed to this spa city to bathe in its mineral waters.

While peacefully soaking in a hot mineral bath, Doolin was surprised one afternoon by Deputy Marshal Bill Tilghman, who leveled a revolver at the naked outlaw and placed him under arrest. A few days later, Doolin was locked in the Guthrie, Oklahoma, jail to await trial for bank robbery. Doolin was convinced that if he was to stand trial that he was certain to be convicted and sent to prison. He calculated that his only chance for freedom was to escape from the Guthrie jail.

During his first week of incarceration, Doolin made friends with the night guard. A week after he was locked up, Doolin told the guard about the fortune in robbery loot that he had buried in a secret location in Kansas. Excited about the prospect of becoming wealthy from the loot he was convinced Doolin would never be able to spend, the guard listened intently to the outlaw's tales of gold coins and thick rolls of currency.

Late one night as the guard made his rounds, Doolin told him that because he would probably never see his buried fortune again, he had decided to give it away. He asked the guard to bring him a piece of paper and a pencil so that he could draw a map to the location of the treasure.

Beside himself with excitement and visions of imminent wealth, the guard abandoned all caution as he hurriedly brought the requested items to Doolin. As the guard handed over the paper and pencil through the cell bars, Doolin grabbed his arm and pulled him sharply up against the iron bars. Applying leverage to the arm of the surprised jailer, Doolin relieved him of his keys and a revolver. Still holding onto the guard, the outlaw opened the cell door. After knocking the guard unconscious, Doolin dragged him into the cell and locked him inside. Exiting the building, Doolin stole a horse and buggy and drove away into the night. He was not seen again for weeks. Most people were convinced that he had retreated to one of his many hideouts in the Osage Hills of eastern Oklahoma, but instead he fled to his place in Burden, where he spent his days counting his money and making plans to retire from banditry, move his wife and child to Kansas, and begin a new life of farming and ranching.

For days, posses of armed deputies combed the Oklahoma countryside in search of the outlaw but were unable to find any trace of him. Eventually, they gave up the search and returned home.

All but one. A lawman named Heck Thomas had gained fame during the preceding years for his tenacity in tracking bandits and bringing them to justice. Thomas had studied Bill Doolin and his habits. He also knew that Doolin was a devoted family man who adored his wife and child. After asking some discrete questions while tracking the escapee through central Oklahoma, Thomas learned that the outlaw's wife and child were currently living with Mrs. Doolin's father near Lawton. Knowing that Doolin would eventually go to his family, Thomas waited patiently and kept a close watch on Mrs. Doolin.

Thomas didn't have long to wait. Within two days of his arrival, Bill Doolin rode the stolen horse and buggy up to the front door of his father-in-law's house. Thomas hid behind a large tree and watched the residence. Two hours later, Doolin, with his wife and child, came out of the house. After throwing several pieces of luggage in the back of the buggy, Doolin helped his family climb aboard and settle into the spring seat. At this point, Thomas stepped from behind the tree and approached the wagon. Doolin spotted the lawman before he had taken two steps and grabbed for a rifle that had been placed under the wagon seat. As he raised the weapon, the outlaw was cut down with a single bullet from Thomas's gun. Doolin fell out of the buggy, dead before he hit the ground.

Anyone who had followed the outlaw career of Bill Doolin knew that he had hidden tens of thousands of dollars' worth of robbery loot. Most suspected it was cached in one or more of his many hideouts in the hills of eastern Oklahoma. Continuous searches over the years, however, failed to locate any of the treasure.

Nearly 20 years after Bill Doolin's death, the identity of his secret hideaway in Burden, Kansas, was discovered. By the time treasure hunters arrived at the location, little could be found of the old house, which had weathered badly and tumbled down, and what was left of the lumber had been scavenged. Weeds and brush had reclaimed most of the yard. While some excavations took place on the property, not a single coin from the fabulous Doolin cache was ever found.

Based on the available evidence, most researchers are convinced that Doolin's treasure still lies in the ground on his property somewhere at Burden. This tiny town of about 500 residents is situated in rolling prairie and farmland. A few of the older residents can still relate stories they heard from parents and grandparents about Bill Doolin seeking refuge here. A few people claim to know exactly where the old Doolin shack once stood, but all admit to some confusion when pressed to identify the site.

Perhaps some dusty and long-ago-filed courthouse documents contain information on the old Doolin property. Some people have suggested that Doolin used an assumed name when he purchased it, making the search even more difficult.

Should the property be located, it is reasonably certain that somewhere near the ruins of the old house an impressive treasure in gold coins taken from long-ago robberies still lies in the ground nearby, the possibility tempting the hopeful.

Chapter 3

Belle Starr's Iron Door Cache

A contemporary of the Daltons and Doolins was the outlaw Belle Starr. Born Myra Belle Shirley in Carthage, Missouri, on February 5, 1848, she grew up with the Jesse James
Gang and members of the Younger gang. The Shirley family,
along with the Jameses and Youngers, were Confederate sym-
pathizers. Following the Civil War, Belle married Jim Reed
and the two had two children, a girl they named Rosie Lee
and nicknamed Pearl and a boy, James Edwin. Jim Reed fell
in with a Cherokee family named Starr and became involved
in horse and cattle theft as well as stagecoach robbery. He
was killed in 1874. In 1880, Belle married Sam Starr. In a
short time, Belle became involved with organizing and planning livestock thefts as well as offering a hideout for outlaws.

By western outlaw standards, Belle Starr was a small-
time criminal and, while colorful, was better known for pro-

viding sanctuary for more famous outlaws such as the James Gang and the Younger Gang.

The story of Belle Starr, like those of many other outlaw figures in American history, has taken on the elements of legend that, as time passes, becomes difficult to distinguish from truth. Much of Starr's life has been documented and told in books and articles. Less is known about her mysterious cache, located somewhere in the Wichita Mountains of southwestern Oklahoma, a trove of U. S. government gold reportedly worth several million dollars in today's values.

Sometime during the 1880s, legend relates that Belle Starr and her gang stopped a freight train bound for the Denver Mint. The train was transporting a cargo of gold ingots destined to be turned into coin. Though the robbery went off without a hitch, the gang was wary of immediate pursuit from federal agents. They decided to cache the loot until things cooled down. Starr settled on a cave in the Wichita Mountains that was known to them. Just before riding away from the scene of the train robbery, gang members removed an iron door, along with its frame, from one of the railroad cars and, using ropes, dragged it along behind them as they made their escape on horseback.

On arriving at the cave, the gold was carried inside and stacked along one wall. The iron door was placed in front of the entrance, then wedged into position and sealed with heavy rocks and mortared. After they secured the door with a substantial and intricate lock, it was covered with brush. Before leaving the area, according to the legend, one of the members of the Belle Starr Gang hammered a railroad spike into an old oak tree located 100 yards from the cave.

During a subsequent train robbery attempt a few months later, all of the gang members save Starr were killed. In 1889,

Starr was gunned down by an as-yet unidentified killer, a crime that has never been solved. With the death of Belle Starr, no one remained alive who knew the exact location of what has come to be known as "the Iron Door Cache."

Railroad detectives learned of the possibility that the stolen gold had been cached in the Wichita Mountains, and though they searched for weeks, they could never find it. With the passage of the years, the matter was forgotten.

During the first decade of the twentieth century, a rancher and his son were riding through a portion of the Wichita Mountains toward the home of some friends who lived in the small town of Indiahoma, located on the south side of the range. After getting a late start, and afraid they might not arrive at their destination before nightfall, they took a little-known shortcut through an unfamiliar part of the range. The trail, they recalled later, skirted Elk Mountain and entered a deep canyon. As they rode along, their attention was captured by the sharp reflection of the setting sun from an object located on the east wall of the canyon. On investigating, they came upon a large, rusted iron door set into a recessed area in the wall. The door was partially covered with rock and debris. They wanted to examine the site further, to see what might lie beyond the odd door, but the father, determined to reach the friend's house before nightfall, insisted they get moving. He promised the boy that they would return soon to see what was behind the door.

Later that evening, when they arrived at their destination, the father described the iron door they found in the canyon and asked if anyone else had ever seen it. Their host grew excited at the news and related the tale of Belle Starr's train robbery and the subsequent caching of the stolen gold shipment as he remembered them. They decided to go in search of it.

Early the next morning, the father, son, and host retraced the path taken the evening before. After entering the canyon, they searched along the east wall but were unable to find the iron door. The host suggested that it might not be the right canyon, so they searched another, then another, but failed to locate the door. Over the next 10 years, the father and son visited the area several more times in search of the iron door but failed to catch even a glimpse of it. They eventually determined that it was likely important to be in a certain location in the canyon at a particular moment during the sunset in order to catch the sun's rays striking the metal object, but they never found themselves in the right canyon at the right time.

In 1908, an elderly woman who gave her name only as Holt arrived in the Wichita Mountains by wagon. She told those she encountered that she had traveled all the way from Missouri and had in her possession a map that allegedly showed the location of the iron door cache. She also carried a large key that, she said, was supposed to unlock the door. When interviewed, she explained how she came into possession of the map and key.

The old woman said that years earlier she had treated the wounds of a dying outlaw who claimed to have been a member of the Belle Starr Gang and to have robbed the gold from the train, cached it in a cave in the Wichita Mountains, and covered the opening with an iron express car door. Before the outlaw died, he sketched a crude map purportedly showing the location of the cave and gave her a key that he said would unlock the large door that covered the entrance. He also told her that not far from the cache was a large oak tree into which had been hammered a railroad spike. The woman had no luck in finding the cache.

In 1910, a group of teenagers was exploring a remote canyon in the Wichita Mountains when they encountered the iron door. Later, one of the boys provided a description of the door and the large rusted padlock that held it shut. The boys assumed the cave behind the door was being used by some local rancher to store feed and supplies, so they left it alone.

After the passage of several years, one of the boys learned the story of Belle Starr's Iron Door Cache. Now a grown man with a family, he was determined to return to the canyon to relocate it. He traveled many times to what he thought was the same canyon, but repeatedly failed to find the iron door. He was convinced that the canyon was located just north of Treasure Lake, the same general area identified by the father and son many years earlier.

During the 1920s, a group of men was hunting raccoons in a remote canyon in the Wichita Mountains. Early one evening, one of their dogs treed a raccoon and a hunter hurried to get a shot at the animal. Just as he was taking aim, he was distracted by a sharp reflection from the opposite wall of the canyon. Curious, he climbed atop a nearby boulder to get a better look at the source of the glare and saw that it was coming from what appeared to be a large metal door set into a recessed portion of the canyon wall. As it was already late afternoon and the hunters had a long way to go to reach their camp site, they left, determined to return another day and investigate the piece of iron.

Six weeks later, the hunters returned to what they believed was the same location but were unable to locate the iron door. Like others who encountered the door, they stated that it was in a canyon not far from Treasure Lake.

Around 1930, three boys were walking through the Wichita Mountains on their way to Indiahoma. In a hurry, they decided to take a shortcut through a canyon that they were convinced would save them some time. As they described it later, the hike through this canyon took them past a large, rusty iron door set into the side of the mountain. The boys climbed up to the strange door and examined it and the large padlock that held it secure. Unaware of the huge fortune in gold ingots that lay just beyond the door, the boys hiked on. In 1981, one of them, now a rancher, heard the story of Belle Starr's Iron Door Cache from a local Indian. Convinced it was the same door he had seen five decades earlier as a boy, the rancher tried to relocate the canyon. Like the others before him who had searched for the iron door, he failed. All he could remember from the early trip with his friends was that the door had been found in a canyon near Treasure Lake.

In 1932, a migrant farm worker was walking from Hobart, Oklahoma, to Lawton in search of work – a journey that took him through the Wichita Mountains. One evening, he made a crude camp, prepared a poor meal of beans and coffee, and fell asleep. The next morning, he continued on his trek and followed a path that took him through a canyon near Elk Mountain. As he passed along the trail, he saw a "rusted door . . . barely exposed on the mountainside." The farm worker was aware of the story of the lost iron door treasure cache and was certain he had found it. He climbed up the slope to the door and strained for nearly an hour trying to get it open. He removed dozens of large rocks from in front of it and uprooted and cleared away a great deal of brush. He finally determined that it would take some heavy tools to break the lock or wedge the huge door from its position in the cave entrance.

Three days later, when he arrived at Lawton, he enlisted the help of two men who supplied the necessary tools, along with some dynamite. When the three returned to the canyon identified by the farm worker, the door could not be found. They searched for a full day, covering the same trail many times, but were unable to relocate the iron door.

During the 1940s, a man named Stephens reported that he had found the iron door. Aware of the story of the lost cache, he immediately recognized the door for what it was. Stephens said he had been hiking in a canyon not far from Treasure Lake when he spotted the door recessed into one side not far from the trail and partially concealed by rocks and brush. He described the door as being one associated with very old railroad cars. He tried to pry the huge door open but with no success. He decided to travel back to his home and return with the tools necessary to remove the door and gain access to the treasure he was certain lay just beyond. Before departing the canyon, he constructed a cairn of rocks at a nearby trail crossing to help him relocate the canyon on his return trip. When Stephens returned several weeks later with tools and a group of men, he could find neither the cairn nor the canyon.

During the 1940s, a rancher was riding through an un-named canyon in the Wichita Mountains in the middle of a summer day when he spotted a large oak tree and decided to take shade under it for a while, resting himself and his horse. While his horse grazed on some nearby grasses, the rancher hung his hat on an old railroad spike that had long ago been hammered into the trunk. He lay down and slept for an hour. Like others who had experienced a close encounter with the iron door treasure, the rancher heard the story of the robbery and the hiding of the gold several years later, along with an allusion to the oak tree with the railroad spike in it. The rancher made several attempts to relocate the canyon but was unsuccessful. He later learned that someone had cut down the oak tree for firewood.

Someday a fortunate treasure hunter will find him or herself in the right canyon just as the setting sun is reflecting off of the iron door set in the mountainside. With luck, the searcher may be able to return to the site with the equipment necessary to pry the door from its setting and recover the fortune in gold ingots lying just inside the cave.

Chapter 4

Black Jack Christian's
Lost Train Robbery Cache

For years, William "Black Jack" Christian was a small-time outlaw who preyed on travelers in and near tiny, out-of-the-way towns in Arizona and New Mexico. He was never known to pull off any significant robberies until November 6, 1897, when he and his partners stopped a train and stole $100,000 worth of gold and silver coins, along with an untold amount of money, watches, and jewelry taken from the passengers. The loot, buried at a location deep in New Mexico's lava beds near the city of Grants, has never been recovered.

William Christian was born in 1871 at Fort Griffin, Texas. Very little is known about his early life, save for the fact that as a young man, he, along with his brother Bob, traveled to New Mexico and became involved in rustling cattle. From cattle rustling, Christian and his gang graduated to robbing banks and trains.

It was a cool, crisp evening in November when the Santa Fe passenger train pulled into the station at Grants, New Mexico. As soon as the train came to a halt, Henry Abel, the train's fireman, jumped down from the engine cab and onto the loading dock to begin his inspection of the locomotive. As Abel was engaged in this activity, Black Jack Christian, along with two accomplices, stepped out from behind the water tower. They wore masks and carried revolvers, each of which was pointed at Abel. As Christian approached the fireman, the other two outlaws raced toward the passenger coaches.

After boarding the coaches, the accomplices went from passenger to passenger and, at gunpoint, demanded that they place their valuables into the large canvas sack the accomplices carried. As this was transpiring, Christian ordered the fireman to pull the train forward one mile. Several minutes later, when the train was halted, Christian had the mail and baggage cars detached and then directed Abel to pull the engine forward another mile. Besides the locomotive, this portion of the train consisted of the tender, the passenger cars, and the express car. At this somewhat remote location, Christian ordered Abel out of the cab and walked him back to the express car, where they were joined by the other two bandits. Christian told Abel to unlock the express car door, but the fireman explained that he did not have a key.

Christian then turned to one of his companions and ordered him to attach a charge of dynamite onto the heavy iron door. Minutes later, the explosion tore apart the entire side of the express car. Still holding Abel at gunpoint, the outlaws entered the wrecked car and located the heavy steel Wells, Fargo safe. Another charge of dynamite was placed on the safe's door, and the subsequent explosion removed it. When the smoke cleared, Christian and his men scooped up over $100,000 in gold and silver coins and placed them in the saddlebags they carried. When the bags were filled, the two outlaws ran toward the nearby trees and retrieved three horses that had been picketed there earlier. After mounting up, Christian thanked Abel for being cooperative and told him goodnight. The three outlaws turned their horses and rode away into the darkness toward the south.

After reporting the robbery to local officials, Abel wired the Santa Fe offices of the railroad company and explained what had happened. He then wired Wells, Fargo and informed them of what had happened to the contents of their safe. The following afternoon, a posse composed of the Cibola County sheriff and several of his deputies, along with railroad detectives and Wells, Fargo agents, departed Grants, rode to the site of the robbery, and picked up the trail of the outlaws. They followed it into the lava beds south of town.

As the lawmen rode into this rough and rocky wilderness, the sheriff explained to the agent and detectives that the lava beds, called malpais by the Mexicans, were a treacherous, rugged, and forbidding landscape composed of ancient, weathered basalt, a rock formed as a result of the cooling of a vast expanse of molten lava from eons-old eruptions in the region. Translated, malpais means "bad country." The lava beds, he explained, were hundreds of feet thick in places, filled with deadly rattlesnakes and occasionally hostile Indians. The trails in the lava beds were narrow, deep, sinuous, and conducive to ambush. Many people who entered the lava beds were never seen again.

Following the robbery of the Santa Fe train, Black Jack Christian and his partners rode hard all night, finally entering the lava beds and following a series of mazelike, narrow, zigzag trails. They eventually arrived at an old Indian campsite deep inside the black expanse of rock. Here they found a fresh water spring and enough grass for their tired mounts to graze. The high basalt walls offered protection from the consistent desiccating winds but, more importantly, they offered an excellent position from which the outlaws could defend themselves from approaching lawmen.

The following morning, following a meal of bacon cooked over a low fire, the three train robbers decided it was time to relax a bit and celebrate their successful robbery. One of them pulled a bottle of whiskey from his saddlebag, opened it, and passed it around. For the next two hours, as the morning sun rose higher in the sky and warmed the small enclosure within the basaltic rocks, the three men imbibed until they were drunk.

Christian walked over to the saddlebags filled with the gold and silver coins and explained how the loot was to be divided. An argument about the split ensued, and with liquor fueling emotions, it soon became violent. One of Christian's henchmen, angered by a comment from the other, pulled his revolver and shot his companion through the head, killing him instantly.

Several hours later when Christian and the surviving partner awoke from a whiskey-induced nap, they decided to bury the dead man. With aching heads and queasy stomachs from their hangovers, the two had just completed the excavation of a shallow hole when they heard the sound of riders in the distance. Christian climbed to an elevated knob, where he could observe the trail without being seen. He spotted the posse less than 100 yards away. Climbing down and hurrying back to the campsite, he told his partner what he had seen and suggested that it was time to make an escape before the lawmen stumbled onto their hiding place. Realizing the importance of haste and not wanting to be encumbered by the heavy saddlebags filled with coins or the canvas sack stuffed with jewelry and watches, they tossed the loot into the hole. Atop the treasure they placed the body of their dead companion. After refilling the excavation, the two men saddled up and fled southward and out of the lava beds.

The posse, composed of 15 men, entered the malpais with optimism, convinced it was only a matter of time before they encountered and captured the outlaws. After three days of fruitless searching, however, they became disheartened, weary, and eager to return to Grants. Little did they realize that they had passed within 100 yards of the train robbers' campsite and that Christian had watched them from his place of concealment. When the posse returned to Grants, a large reward was offered for Black Jack Christian, dead or alive.

The next morning, after riding all night, Christian suggested that he and his partner separate and each go his own way to confuse any pursuing lawmen. They agreed to meet in 30 days at a tavern in Silver City, New Mexico. From there, Christian suggested they would quietly return to the lava beds and retrieve the treasure.

Two weeks later, Christian, along with three companions, robbed a pair of stagecoaches in Arizona. Lawmen took pursuit and caught up with the bandits in a narrow canyon. A gunfight ensued, and all four of the outlaws were mortally wounded. They were loaded into a lumber wagon and hauled to the nearest town, where their bodies were placed on display. That location is called Black Jack Canyon to this day. (A second version of what happened to Christian relates that, badly wounded, he was transported to a clinic in Silver City, where he survived for two more days before dying.)

About the time Christian died, his surviving partner attempted to rob another train in eastern Arizona. He was captured, tried, found guilty, and sentenced to 20 years in the Territorial Prison at Yuma. He died from tuberculosis after serving only five years. No one was left alive who knew the location of the buried train robbery loot in the lava beds south of Grants, New Mexico.

During the month of July 1914, an out-of-work cowboy was traveling from Grants to Silver City in search of employment and attempted a shortcut through the lava beds. Sundown found him entering a small grassy opening encircled by the high black volcanic rock. There was sufficient grass for his horse and at one end of the sward he found a freshwater spring. After filling his canteen, he built a small campfire and was boiling water for coffee when he spotted a low mound of dirt not far from where he squatted. It resembled a grave, but he wasn't certain. Curious, he took a stick and dug into the mound. Just inches below the surface, he encountered a human skeleton and some rotted clothing. Unnerved by the discovery, he quickly refilled the hole and returned to the campfire.

Unknown to the itinerant cowboy, a fortune in gold and silver coins as well as money, jewelry, and watches reposed beneath the grisly skeleton. Had he dug only a few inches further, he would have been rewarded with a treasure that would have exceeded his wildest dreams, and he would never have had to face the rugged and often poverty-laced life of a cowhand again. Years later, when the cowboy was an old man with grandchildren, he learned the story of the robbery of the Santa Fe train by the outlaw Black Jack Christian and the subsequent caching of the gold and silver coins and jewelry in the malpais. The old cowboy realized that he had accidentally stumbled upon the location of the cache during his trek through the lava beds decades earlier.

Over the next two years, the old man undertook several trips into the rugged lava beds in an attempt to relocate the same little grassy campsite, the one with the freshwater spring and the low mound of dirt, but he never found it.

Today Black Jack Christian's train robbery loot is estimated to be worth in excess of $2 million. The lava beds where the treasure was cached are now the El Malpais National Monument. Those who have searched for this treasure have reported that there exist in this challenging landscape not one but many such grassy, spring-fed environments. One of them, however, contains the skeleton of a train robber and a huge fortune just a few inches below the surface.

Chapter 5

Black Jack Ketchum and His Silver Coin Cache

It can be argued that the criminal business of train robbery attracted the likes of people who were predestined for outlaw fame, fearless and daring people who possessed a sense of adventure. It can likewise be argued that the successful train robberies themselves generated the notoriety and recognition for which many well-known bad people have been associated: Frank and Jesse James, Butch Cassidy and the Sundance Kid, Sam Bass, Rube Burrow, and others all held reputations as daring and successful train robbers.

Black Jack Christian was not the only outlaw who went by the nickname "Black Jack." A lesser-known train robber than the James brothers and Butch Cassidy, but no less effective, was Thomas Edward "Black Jack" Ketchum, regarded by many as a significant and dangerous outlaw scourge of the

American west. Ketchum, along with his brother, Sam, were well-known to lawmen throughout much of Wyoming and Colorado but during most of their criminal careers never gained reputations like those accorded to James, Cassidy, and others.

Thomas Ketchum was born near China Creek on October 31, 1863, in San Saba County in the northern part of the Texas Hill Country. (At least one report says he was born in 1866.) Ketchum's father died when he was only five years old, and his mother, who was blind, passed away when he was 10. Tom's older brother, Green Berry Ketchum, became a successful rancher and breeder of horses in the area. Another brother, Sam, married and fathered two children. When Tom decided to depart the family fold and travel west to try to make it on his own, Sam left his family and joined him. Initially, the two men found work as ranch hands in West Texas and northern New Mexico and participated in a number of cattle drives into Colorado and Wyoming.

By 1892, Tom and Sam had committed themselves to a life of outlawry. Along with several other members of what was referred to as the "Black Jack Ketchum Gang," they held up and robbed an Atchison, Topeka & Santa Fe train near Deming, New Mexico. They got away with an estimated $20,000. To Ketchum, train robbery was clearly more lucrative than cowboying.

Over the next several years, Tom and Sam Ketchum, while occasionally finding work on cattle ranches, preferred instead to pursue their criminal activities, finding them more rewarding and more adventurous. They and/or their gang members were responsible for several murders and train robberies.

Oddly, both Tom and Sam were referred to as "Black Jack" at various times, often generating a level of confusion among researchers relative to which brother participated in which holdup and to what degree. Though it has been written that both were involved in a number of train robberies together, there is little on record to substantiate the claim. At times, both Tom and Sam Ketchum rode with Butch Cassidy, Elzy Lay, Harry Longabaugh, and other members of the Wild Bunch, noted and proficient train robbers themselves. There is little doubt that the brothers learned much about the criminal trade from Cassidy and other gang members. When not riding with the Wild Bunch, Black Jack, sometimes accompanied by his brother and other gang members he had recruited, went out on their own to indulge in robbing sprees. By late 1895, former Wild Bunch member Harvey "Kid Curry" Logan had become a member of Black Jack's gang.

Of the two brothers, Tom Ketchum was the most recognized and, in the end, generated the most publicity and notoriety. Ketchum was regarded by most who were acquainted with him as "crazy," often exhibiting behavior that was considered bizarre even by the standards held by most hardened outlaws. Today Ketchum would be referred to as a psychopath. The clearly deranged Ketchum was considered far too outrageous, dangerous, and unpredictable even for most of the members of the Wild Bunch, themselves no strangers to violent men, killing, and related activity.

On more than one occasion, Ketchum was observed beating himself over the head with his own revolver and lashing himself across the neck and back with his lariat, self-inflicted punishment for some mistake he had determined was his fault. Once, when a woman he had been seeing decided she wanted nothing to do with him, Ketchum, in front of gang members, beat himself bloody with the butt of his revolver.

Black Jack Ketchum was also known to drink heavily. Sometimes by himself and at other times with companions, he would remain drunk for long periods of time, the alcohol making him more belligerent, bellicose, and aggressive than he normally was.

It was just a matter of time before Black Jack Ketchum returned to his home state of Texas to rob a train. On May 14, 1897, Thomas "Black Jack" Ketchum, along with two unidentified companions, robbed a Southern Pacific train near the remote and lonely Lozier Station in the Big Bend Country of West Texas and 250 straight-line miles west of San Antonio. Though unidentified, it is believed by many that one of Ketchum's partners was Ben Kilpatrick. Kilpatrick had previous train robbery experience as a member of the Wild Bunch. Years later, Kilpatrick would return to that part of West Texas to attempt another robbery of this same train. It would prove to be his last successful heist.

At 2:00 a.m. on the morning of May 10, the Southern Pacific Sunset Limited made an emergency stop at the unmanned Lozier siding. Less than an hour earlier, the train had pulled out of Del Rio, near the Mexican border, and was westbound for El Paso. Several minutes after leaving Del Rio, the engineer, a man named Freese, told the conductor, named Burns, that the train was running erratically. Since the next station down the line was Lozier, Freese recommended that they stop there and try to determine the problem. After pulling into the station, Freese and the conductor examined the train in an attempt to locate the disturbance. As the men were thus occupied, the fireman topped off the water tank from the supply positioned next to the tracks.

Several dozen yards behind the engine, coal tender, and at least one passenger car was the express car. Wells, Fargo messenger Henry Boyce was in the final stages of conducting an inventory of the shipment that had been placed on board at Del Rio. The shipment consisted of over $90,000 in paper currency and a bit more than $6,000 in silver coins. Boyce carefully placed the shipment into the safe, which was then closed and locked.

Engineer Freese descended from the cab in the dark, walked around the locomotive, and examined it, trying to determine the source of the problem. He was accompanied by conductor Burns. As the two men went about their inspection, three men observed their movements from the deep shadows of the station building a short distance away. One of the men was Ketchum. By this time, Ketchum was a well-known, and wanted, outlaw who made his reputation as a train robber in Colorado and Wyoming. Because of continual scrapes with the law in those states, as well as the fact that he was heavily pursued, Ketchum had drifted south with his gang into Texas where he was less known.

It took Freese and Burns an hour to detect the problem with the engine and correct it. Shortly after climbing back into the locomotive, the engineer gave the signal to proceed and the train was under way. As the train began the slow departure from the station, and before it picked up momentum, the outlaws struck. Ketchum, carrying a knapsack and a rifle and accompanied by one of his partners, dashed from their hiding place and leaped onto one of the railroad cars. The two men climbed the ladder to the roof and made their way over several more cars toward the engine.

As Ketchum and his companion were making their way forward, the outlaw remaining behind cut the telegraph wire that connected this station to others down the line. This done, he dashed several dozen yards away and down into a shallow

$90,000 in currency was left untouched. Ketchum checked his watch and noted that 90 minutes had passed since the train had pulled away from the Lozier station. A moment later, the third outlaw arrived with the horses. After tying the coin-filled knapsack behind his saddle, the always-unpredictable Ketchum bade a polite goodbye to Freese, Burns, Bochat, and Boyce and, along with his two companions, rode away toward the southwest, in the direction of the Chisos Mountains.

As Ketchum and his gang disappeared into the desert darkness, Freese raced back to the engine and in a short time had the train barreling toward the next stop – Sanderson. On pulling into the station, conductor Burns leaped out of the cab and informed the agent of what had happened at Lozier. He instructed the agent to telegraph news of the robbery to Southern Pacific Railroad authorities in El Paso immediately.

By the time the sun had come up, Texas Ranger Captain John R. Hughes had received word of the robbery. From the ranger encampment at Ysleta, Texas, some 15 miles downriver from El Paso, Hughes handpicked a platoon of 15 rangers, armed them, and supplied them with provisions to last at least a week. After assembling a string of strong and trail-hardened mounts, the rangers set out toward the robbery site.

When the Texas Ranger contingent rode up to the scene of the robbery, they found enough signs to indicate that the robbers had fled toward the southwest. After following the tracks for a short distance, however, the rangers lost them. For several days, Hughes and company searched the rugged arid country just south of the robbery site, but to no avail – they were unable to find the trail of the bandits. On the fourth day, as they were circling a potential area, one of the rangers came across the tracks of three horses heading south-westward. The rangers followed the trail but lost it again, this time when it crossed a stretch of granite outcrop. For another full week, the rangers crisscrossed the area in hope of relo-cating the tracks of the outlaws but were unsuccessful. Cap-tain Hughes finally called a halt to the search and returned with his charges to Ysleta.

After fleeing the robbery site, Ketchum and his compan-ions had ridden hard for two days and nights, stopping only to water and rest the horses. On the morning of the third day of flight, the gang had made its way deep into the remote and barely accessible reaches of the Big Bend Country, not far from the Mexican border. Two more days of riding through deep canyons and across rugged ridges brought them to their planned destination: the isolated ranch of the Reagan brothers in Reagan Canyon.

The relationship between the four Reagan brothers and the outlaw Black Jack Ketchum was longstanding. The ranch-ers agreed to allow Ketchum and his gang hide out in the area for a few days. As the train robbers unsaddled their horses, one of the ranch hands obliterated their tracks into the ranch by driving a herd of cattle over them.

Ketchum was concerned that the Texas Rangers would be searching for them and might be closing in on their hide-out. It was just a matter of time, he reasoned, before they ar-rived. Not wanting to be caught with the $6,000 in silver coins and fearing that if he transported them in his saddle-bags the extra weight would slow him down, Ketchum de-cided to cache the loot at some location on the ranch. After giving the Reagan brothers $200, Ketchum stuffed the re-maining coins into his knapsack and carried them to a cave he had located earlier a short distance north of Reagan

Canyon. The next day, the three outlaws rode away, intending to return at some future date and retrieve the treasure. None of them could have realized that they would never see that part of Texas again.

Ketchum decided it was in his best interest to put as much distance as possible between himself and the Texas Rangers, so he traveled to Colorado. Once he had settled into the Rocky Mountain state, the outlaw lost no time in returning to robbing trains.

On September 3, 1897, Ketchum and his gang robbed a Colorado & Southern train, making off with $3,500. On July 11, 1899, the gang struck again, robbing the same train and taking $70,000 in gold coins. It was to be the last successful robbery undertaken by Ketchum.

Following the July 11 robbery, Huerfano County (Colorado) sheriff Farr assembled a posse consisting of nine men experienced in tracking and fighting. They were accompanied by two railroad detectives. A few days later the posse caught up with the robbers and a gunfight ensued. Two members of the gang were killed and Black Jack's brother Sam was wounded. Black Jack, along with Bill Franks and another man, named McGinnis, escaped.

Sam Ketchum was arrested. While waiting for trial in a Santa Fe, New Mexico, jail, he contracted blood poisoning, presumably from his wound, and died. Franks was killed in San Angelo, Texas, in 1901. McGinnis was later captured, tried, and sentenced to the New Mexico penitentiary. He was pardoned in 1906.

Though his gang had been decimated and he had suffered significant failure, Thomas "Black Jack" Ketchum was more determined than ever to return to robbing trains. His next attempt turned out to be his last.

On April 16, 1899, near Folsom, New Mexico, Black Jack Ketchum attempted to rob the Colorado & Southern train for the third time. After spending the night in a nearby cave, he rode to the railroad station at Folsom, boarded the train from the blind side of the baggage car, and made his way to the coal tender.

After the train had traveled about three miles from the station, Ketchum jumped into the locomotive cab from the coal tender, to the surprise of the engineer, and ordered the train stopped. The outlaw's plan was to disconnect the express and mail cars from the rest of the train and have the engineer proceed another mile up the track. There, the train was to be stopped once more and Ketchum would proceed to the express and mail cars, where he intended to retrieve the money. The train robber erred, however, in determining the location for the train to stop. It was on a curve that left the train in a cramped position where, as it turned out, it was impossible to uncouple the cars.

After the train stopped, Ketchum made his way to the cars he had targeted. Some have recorded that the always-volatile Ketchum, after entering the express car, shot the express messenger in the jaw. Others say this did not happen.

The conductor, Frank Harrington, had lost his patience with train robbers. His train had already been robbed three times, and he was determined that it would not happen again. He grabbed a shotgun and went after Ketchum. Harrington found Ketchum inside the baggage car and pointed the weapon at him. Reflexively, Ketchum got off a hurried shot at the conductor, barely missing him. (One report states that the conductor was struck by the bullet). At about the same time, Harrington fired one of the barrels of the scattergun he was carrying, a load of buckshot striking Ketchum in the left elbow, destroying his lower arm and nearly severing it. The impact knocked the outlaw out of the express car and onto the ground. Harrington shouted for the engineer to get the train moving as fast as possible.

Bleeding heavily, Ketchum ran toward his horse. As he later explained to his interrogators, he tried a dozen times to climb into the saddle but was too weak to manage. Dizzy from the effort and loss of blood, he collapsed to the ground and decided to wait for the inevitable posse to arrive.

The engineer stopped the Colorado & Southern train at every station he came to, each time having telegraphs sent to various law enforcement agencies reporting the robbery and advising them to be on the lookout for a badly wounded man who was likely still near the scene of the attempted holdup. A short time later, the train pulled into the station at Clayton, New Mexico, where the engineer reported the attempted holdup to the sheriff. Posses were formed and raced back to the robbery site, but no sign of Ketchum could be found.

Fearing that he would bleed to death from his wound, Ketchum managed to flag down another train. When the train stopped, the brakeman climbed down from the cab and approached the stranger, who appeared to be in great pain. As he neared, Ketchum drew his revolver and pointed it at him. The conductor was quoted as saying, "We just came to help you, but if this is the way you feel we will go and leave you."

Ketchum lowered his weapon and told the brakeman that he was "all done," and to "take me in." He was placed in the caboose, helped to a cot, and carried into Folsom. He was later placed under arrest by Union County sheriff Saturnino Pinard.

At his arrest, Ketchum gave his name as Frank Stevens. (At least one writer claimed that the name he gave was

George Stevens). His wound was patched up as well as could be managed. Forty-two shotgun pellets were removed from the damaged arm. Later, Ketchum was taken to the San Rafael Hospital at Trinidad, Colorado, where his wounded arm was amputated.

As the investigation proceeded, it was soon learned that the name "Stevens" was an alias and that the man who sat before the investigators was none other than the notorious train robber Black Jack Ketchum. It was also learned that Ketchum was wanted in four other states for murder, robbery, and other crimes. When he was well enough to travel, Ketchum was transported to Santa Fe for "safekeeping."

While Black Jack Ketchum was in custody in Santa Fe, detectives and other officials arrived to question him about the robbery of the Southern Pacific Sunset Limited near Lozier Station in West Texas. Ketchum admitted his role in the robbery and provided details.

Ketchum also described his long flight southwestward into the arid Big Bend country and hiding out at the Reagan brothers' ranch. Ketchum even confessed to caching the knapsack filled with silver coins in a remote cave located on the ranch. The coins, he informed them, were still there because he had not had an opportunity to return for them, and the two companions who had accompanied him at the time were dead. When the lawmen asked for specific directions to the cave, Ketchum refused to give them any.

The now-one-armed Black Jack Ketchum was returned to Clayton, New Mexico, where he was formally charged. He was tried, found guilty, and sentenced to be hanged. Ketchum was given an opportunity to make a confession to a priest. Instead, he told the holy man, "I'm gonna die as I've lived. And you ain't gonna change me in a few minutes." Then he smiled and said, "Have someone play a fiddle when I swing off."

At 8:00 a.m. on the cool morning of April 26, 1901, Thomas "Black Jack" Ketchum was marched to the gallows. He was manacled and a heavy steel belt encircled his waist. His left arm was cuffed to the belt, and his legs were linked together with a short length of chain. He was also surrounded by several armed lawmen. The reason for applying these seemingly unnecessary precautions to a one-armed and heavily shackled prisoner were related to a rumor that some of his gang members might arrive and try to free him.

Within minutes after Ketchum had ascended the steps to the gallows, a rope was placed around his neck and a black hood placed over his head. The hood was pinned to his shirt.

As he was being readied for his execution, Ketchum taunted his captors, saying, "Hurry up, boys; get this over with." The outlaw was also credited with stating, "I'll be in hell before you start breakfast, boys!" Following some final adjustments to the noose, Ketchum yelled, "Let 'er rip!"

Clayton Sheriff Garcia needed two blows from a hatchet to sever the rope that released the trapdoor on which Ketchum stood. As it swung open, Ketchum dropped through the opening. When his body reached the end of the rope, his head was snapped off of the torso. The head remained inside the black hood. One writer said that the only thing keeping it from rolling away was the fact that the hood had been pinned to the shirt. This seems unlikely; if the force was strong enough to tear the head from the body, it surely would have torn the hood away from where it was pinned to the shirt. Another writer wrote that the body separated from the head and then the head fell down on top of the torso after it swung loose from the rope. Photographs were then taken of the head and the decapitated body. Ketchum was later buried in the new Clayton cemetery.

Decapitations in this manner were unheard of in formal executions of the time. A number of explanations for this unusual occurrence have been offered, including (1) that the gallows was too high and the subsequent speed attained by the body while falling was sufficient to separate it from the head; (2) that the noose was too tight; and (3) that the rope was too thin for such a heavy man and thus cut through his flesh and bone. Some even suggested that the decapitation had been arranged on purpose, though no evidence for such a theory was ever advanced.

Black Jack Ketchum's outlaw life has been told and retold in books, articles, and films. Lacking the charm and glamor of other notorious outlaws and train robbers of the day, such as Butch Cassidy, Jesse James, and others, Ketchum is simply regarded by most researchers as a crazed robber and killer. Black Jack was the only man ever subjected to capital punishment in the state of New Mexico for "felonious assault upon a railway train."

Black Jack Ketchum had a long and colorful, albeit criminal, life journey after leaving his home in San Saba County, Texas. His travels took him throughout much of the American West, his ambitions carrying him through one outlaw escapade after another.

The silver coins Black Jack Ketchum took from the Southern Pacific Railroad near Lozier, Texas, and cached in a remote cave in southwest Texas are still searched for to this day.

Chapter 6

Sam Bass's Outlaw Treasure

Like many American outlaws, Sam Bass has achieved the status of legend. A daring holdup man who met his end in a shootout with lawmen, Bass has had streets named after him, has been portrayed in films, and is touted as a colorful desperado. Bass was one of several notorious outlaws who operated out of Texas during the late 1800s. Following a series of robberies and the accumulation of thousands of dollars in gold coins and jewelry, the famed outlaw buried his wealth in Denton County, Texas, where most of it remains to this day. Like those of many famous outlaws, the story of Sam Bass mixes legend with fact, but there remains enough documented evidence about his escapades to validate his reputation as a cunning and efficient outlaw and a clever and successful train and stagecoach robber.

Deputy Moore that Bass carried a holstered revolver under his coat. Moore immediately alerted another deputy nearby, A. M. Grimes, and together the two lawmen followed the gang members into the store.

Although Moore and Grimes had been advised that Sam Bass and his gang were likely to be in the area, the two lawmen did not recognize the outlaw. While Moore waited outside, Grimes approached Bass in the store, placed a hand over the bulge in his coat, and asked the newcomer if he was carrying a weapon. In response, Bass yanked his revolver from its holster and shot Grimes. As the startled deputy stumbled back toward the front door and collapsed, Moore drew his handgun and fired at Bass, striking the outlaw in the right hand and damaging his middle and ring fingers. A second later, the three train robbers fled the store, firing at deputy Moore as they ran. Moore was struck in the chest but continued shooting at the gang members.

At the first sound of the shooting at Koppel's Store, the Texas Rangers gathered and raced to the scene. Spotting the fleeing Bass, Barnes, and Jackson, they opened fire. Ranger George Harrell took careful aim and shot Bass, the bullet striking him one inch to the left of his spinal column. Bass staggered and dropped to the ground.

Seaborn Barnes, who had been running alongside Bass, was struck in the head and was likely dead before he hit the ground. Frank Jackson paused in his flight long enough to assist Bass to his feet and thence onto his horse. At the same time, the plucky Jackson kept up a steady fire at the Texas Rangers, who were rapidly closing in.

Once mounted, Jackson and the badly wounded Bass spurred their horses hard and rode out of Round Rock toward the north. It was all Bass could do to stay in the saddle. He lost his grip and almost fell off his horse several times. Once out of sight of their pursuers, the two outlaws turned west into a dense oak woods.

Weakened from intense pain and loss of blood, Bass finally fell from his saddle. Jackson bandaged the leader's wounds as best he could, pulled him a short distance off the trail, and tried to make him comfortable. Bass encouraged his partner to leave him, to escape. At first Jackson refused, but was soon talked into mounting his horse and riding away. Sam Bass was now left to fend for himself. Writhing in severe pain, the outlaw lay on the ground near Brush Creek all night long, too weak to continue his flight.

By dawn, Bass had lost a considerable amount of blood. Unable to stand, he crawled away from his hiding place. After covering almost a half-mile, and in severe agony, he arrived at a location where a new spur of the International and Great Northern Railroad was being constructed. Several railroad workers engaged in laying track spotted Bass, barely alive, but continued with their work. They were too far away to discern that the man was badly wounded.

A short time later a squad of Texas Rangers searching throughout the area arrived at the railroad construction site. They spotted Bass lying still and quiet beneath a live oak tree but mistook him for one of the railroad workers taking a nap. As the rangers approached, Bass raised an arm and said, "Don't shoot. I'm Sam Bass." The rangers transported the outlaw to Round Rock and placed him in the care of a physician, though it was clear he would not live long.

Texas Ranger Major John B. Jones sat beside Bass in the doctor's office during most of his remaining time. Jones interrogated Bass about his gang members and tried to learn some information about where they might have gone into hiding. Bass was too weak to converse and fell asleep.

The next morning Jones once again took a seat next to the dying Bass and questioned him further. Bass provided a bit of information on only the members of the gang who had been killed, but none at all on the survivors. After several minutes of conversation, Bass fell silent for a while, then closed his eyes as if to sleep. A few moments later he opened them and looked around as if confused and frightened. He said, "The world is a-bobbin' around." Those were his last words. Sam Bass died the following day, July 21. It was his 27th birthday. He was buried in the Round Rock cemetery, next to Seaborn Barnes.

Following the demise of Sam Bass, people began to wonder about the wealth that they believed he had accumulated. Some who were in sympathy with the outlaw claimed he had given most of it to the poor and the needy. This Robin Hood image often attributed to Bass had some basis in fact, for he was given to helping the underprivileged. There was also a large number of people who were convinced that Bass was little more than a ruthless outlaw who gambled away most of the money he stole.

Most, however, were convinced that Bass hid his wealth in a shallow cave in or near Cove Hollow. This may be true, or partly true. There is evidence that Bass may have split up his treasure and cached portions of it in at least four different locations at or near his North Texas hideout.

During the first decade of the twentieth century, a farmer named Henry Chapman found what many believe was part of Sam Bass's treasure. Chapman owned a small farm near Springtown in Williamson County. One day, as Chapman was riding through the woods between Clear Fork Creek and Salt Creek, his mule began acting contrary. The farmer dismounted to check the girth on the balky animal, and as he was tightening it, he noticed a low mound of dirt just off the trail. At first, he believed it to be a grave, but closer examination revealed that it was not.

Chapman dug into the mound and was surprised to discover a bushel-sized wooden box filled to the top with gold and silver coins. All of the gold coins bore the date 1877. Except for these, none of the rest of Sam Bass's 1877 gold coins ever appeared in circulation, supporting the belief that the rest of his treasure is still buried intact somewhere in North Texas, awaiting discovery by some fortunate treasure hunter.

Chapter 7

Outlaw John Glanton and His Buried Fortune at Fort Defiance

Tales of America's outlaws are replete with accounts of shootings and shootouts. Indeed, guns were fired and blood spilled on numerous occasions such as bank and train robberies and encounters with lawmen. While such things did happen, the truth is that most of the tales are exaggerated and many outlaws have been credited with far more killings than they actually committed. One exception is John Glanton. During his lifetime, Glanton acquired a reputation as a ruthless and cunning bandit and scalp-hunter, and his victims numbered into the dozens, if not the hundreds. Of all of America's outlaws, Glanton may have been the most bloodthirsty.

Unlike most outlaws, Glanton possessed a remarkable ability to hold on to his wealth, an impressive fortune gleaned from numerous robberies. Glanton lived frugally, carefully saved his money, and carried it with him everywhere he traveled. After 10 years of banditry, along with a number of crooked business practices, Glanton had amassed a large fortune that he buried only a few hours before his death. For more than a century, people have searched for this treasure, but Glanton's cache has never been found.

John Joel Glanton was born in 1819 in Edgefield County, South Carolina. As a youth he left home and wandered to Central and West Texas where, at 17 years of age, was hired as an army scout for Lieutenant James Fannin. Weeks later, Glanton left his job, took an Apache bride, and settled on a small farm near the Guadalupe River in Gonzalez County, Texas. After being married only a few months, Glanton returned home from a hunting trip to find his wife murdered and scalped, presumably by Comanches.

After burying his wife, Glanton moved to San Antonio, where he remarried, this time to a young lady from a well-to-do Mexican family. During the winter of 1847, however, he abandoned her and enlisted as a private in the U. S. Army. Military records show that Glanton participated in the Snively Expedition, spent time under the command of General Zachary Taylor, and served with Captain Jack Hayes in the war with Mexico. As a soldier, Glanton earned a reputation for being boisterous and ready to fight at a moment's notice. In 1848, while on duty in Mexico, he was arrested for shooting a native during a barroom brawl. One week later, he broke out of jail, deserted the army, and fled deep into the Mexican state of Chihuahua.

Several months later, Glanton reappeared as a member of a band of scalp-hunters working for the Mexican government. Because of repeated conflict between the Mexicans and the Apaches, Glanton and his fellows were promised $50 in gold for each Apache scalp they brought in. Fearless and ferocious, this small army attacked dozens of Apache encampments, killing men, women, and children in their grisly quest. When they were unable to find Indians, these predators lifted the scalps of Mexicans and passed them off as Apaches. When government officials in Chihuahua learned of this, they chased the band northward across the Rio Grande into Texas. During the flight, Glanton and Santiago Kirker, the leader of the group, had a violent argument. During the ensuing knife fight, according to legend, Glanton killed Kirker and assumed leadership of the group of scalp-hunters.

Glanton led the band into the Mexican state of Sonora, located west of Chihuahua, and made arrangements with military and government officials there to bring in more Apache scalps. The scalp-hunters ranged far and wide in their search for Indians, killing and scalping hundreds. Their journeys sometimes took them into New Mexico, where, in addition to hunting Apaches, they raided and looted small villages as well as robbing stagecoaches and wagons.

As the band accumulated booty, the always-frugal Glanton took to packing his share onto mules he brought along for that purpose. It was said that he no longer slept at night but preferred to stand guard over his gold. It was also during this time that Glanton began to change.

Where before Glanton killed Indians and took scalps because it was a way to make a living, he now became obsessed with murder and took great pleasure in it. In addition to killing Indians and Mexicans, he would shoot or stab anyone who disagreed with him. He often shot travelers he encountered along the roads just for the sport of it. Glanton also began to drink excessively and gamble frequently. In the meantime, he continued to amass great wealth and now required several mules to transport it all.

Glanton's depredations took him and his band into Arizona, and they settled into a camp south of Tucson. The group of cutthroats numbered 14, half of whom were Mexican. The men made frequent raids on nearby mining camps and often attacked freight wagons. In the process, they collected thousands of dollars' worth of gold nuggets. When a group of vigilantes attacked their camp, Glanton led his men north and east to Phoenix, in search of more opportunities for raiding. They had not been in the area long when they came upon and attacked a Pima Indian village for the purpose of taking scalps. The Indians were well-armed, however, and during the ensuing battle, half of Glanton's forces were killed or wounded. While retreating from the Indians, Glanton reportedly shot and killed the wounded members of his band so they would not slow down the escape.

The survivors continued to ride westward and, in a few weeks, arrived at the small town of Yuma, near the Colorado River. In a short time, Glanton and his men took over the town and seized the two ferryboats that transported goods and travelers across the river to and from California. Glanton believed he could become even wealthier in Yuma, so he ordered the construction of an adobe-walled fortress on a hill in the town overlooking the river. He and his men took mistresses from the Mexican population and all moved into the fortress that Glanton named Fort Defiance. From here, he managed the ferryboat operation as well as a saloon and several other businesses in town.

Men returning from the gold fields in California were systematically robbed and killed on the ferry and their bodies tossed into the current. In this manner Glanton piled up more gold and currency until he became what many believe to be one of the wealthiest men in the Southwest. As he grew richer, observers were convinced he was growing more insane. His men, desperadoes of the first order, became cautious, even fearful, of his wild and unpredictable manner. One by one, they deserted him.

Eventually, Glanton found himself alone, with only his fortune to keep him company. He remained locked inside Fort Defiance for weeks at a time, rarely making appearances in town. On the few occasions that he was seen on the streets of Yuma, he bore the look of a depraved maniac, with long, stringy, and unkempt hair, wearing filthy ragged clothes, and bearing a frightening look in his eyes. In one hand he carried a pistol, in the other, a large Bowie knife.

One day Glanton learned that a large band of Yuma Indians was approaching Fort Defiance, intent on attacking it. The Yumas had earlier operated a ferry downriver from Glanton's business. Not wishing for any competition, Glanton and a handful of recently recruited men had attacked the Indians, killing several, and sank their boat. On learning that Glanton's small army no longer supported him, it is likely that the Indians became bent on revenge. Glanton was convinced they were after his fortune and he was determined to hide it. During the day and well into the night, Glanton worked feverishly, hiding his treasure of American and Mexican gold coins, gold nuggets, and currency. Some claim Glanton never left the safety of Fort Defiance and that he buried his wealth somewhere within the confines of the adobe fortress. Others maintain that Glanton made several trips into the nearby sand hills and hid his fortune there.

The Indians attacked at dawn on April 23, 1850. They burned down much of the town of Yuma, killing several of its citizens. Encountering no resistance, they stormed Fort Defiance and set fire to the structures within. After the Indians departed, several surviving Yuma citizens entered the fortress and found Glanton's body. It had been scalped and horribly mutilated. A search of the fortress for his treasure yielded nothing.

As the news of Glanton's death spread throughout the territory, dozens of men arrived to search for the treasure they knew to be buried somewhere in or near the walled fort. Hundreds of holes were excavated inside the enclosure, pitting nearly every square foot of the ground, but nothing of value was found. Holes were likewise dug for miles out into the desert in all directions from the town and the fort, but no cache of treasure was encountered.

An old-timer who took over the operation of the ferry befriended an aged Yuma Indian several years after the raid. The ferryman learned that the Indian had participated in the attack on the town and the fort. When he asked the Indian if he knew anything about Glanton's treasure, the Yuma related a curious story. He said that he and several other Yuma warriors had observed Glanton making several trips from the fort with his mules laden with gold and that they had watched as he dug several holes in the sand dunes south of town, in which he buried his wealth. When Glanton returned to the fort for the last time, the Indians advanced on the site, dug up the gold and money, and threw it all into the swirling waters of the Colorado River.

Chapter 8

Tiburcio Vasquez and the
500-Pound Silver Ingot

During the 1870s, several roads leading into and out of the southern California city of Los Angeles were constantly terrorized by the Mexican bandit Tiburcio Vasquez and his ruthless gang of outlaws. Vasquez, who was accompanied by selected murderers and thieves, preyed on travelers and freight wagons, often leaving his robbery victims lying in the desert sand, riddled with bullets or hanging from a nearby tree.

Vasquez started his life of crime rustling horses. He was captured and sentenced to five years in prison at San Quentin. Upon release, he lost no time in returning to rustling livestock. To this, he added robbing stores, stage-coaches, and freight wagons. Despite his tendencies toward crime, Vasquez was an ardent defender of Mexican American rights, and to this day is regarded as a hero among that ethnic group. It is believed that Vasquez was the inspiration for the fictional bandit-hero character Zorro.

One day in 1872, Vasquez and his band attacked a freight wagon and absconded with two 500-pound silver ingots, one of which remains hidden to this day in the hills north of Los Angeles.

During Nevada's glory days in the gold and silver mining boom of the mid-nineteenth century, William M. Stewart made a fortune. One of his major investments was the famed Comstock Lode, from which he profited nicely. Stewart, an ambitious man who possessed a flair for politics as well as mining and business, was eventually elected to the Nevada Senate.

In 1872, Stewart visited his brother Robert in Panamint, California, and together the two joined forces to obtain and operate a rich silver mine located in the nearby mountains. About once every six weeks, a shipment of silver bullion was sent from the mine, via pack mules, to Los Angeles, approximately 150 miles to the south. While other miners and shippers suffered depredations at the hands of Tiburcio Vasquez and his gang, the Stewart mining enterprise had yet to be attacked by the gang. One day, however, as the Stewart brothers prepared a shipment, they received word that Vasquez was waiting along the trail to hold up the pack train.

William Stewart decided to wait for several days before sending out the pack train, in the hope that the bandit would grow weary of waiting and depart. Three days later, Stewart learned that because the pack train was not forthcoming, Vasquez had decided to conduct a raid on the mine instead. This information bothered Stewart, for while Vasquez would no doubt be accompanied by nearly a dozen fearless bandits, only six unarmed Chinese laborers were available to defend the mine.

Stewart, normally a calm man, became frustrated at this turn of events, for following the delivery of this particular shipment of silver, he had intended to offer the mine for sale to a group of Los Angeles investors. If the potential buyers learned of outlaw hostilities in the area, they would likely back off from the purchase. Stewart came up with an idea he believed might discourage the bandits.

Stewart had 1,000 pounds of silver bullion packed and ready for shipment. The bullion consisted of dozens of small ingots that were to be distributed onto several mules. Stewart ordered the silver to be brought into the furnace room, where he arranged for his employees to construct a large ingot mold. They were instructed to melt the smaller ingots and pour the molten ore into the new mold. Two new ingots were formed, each one weighing 500 pounds. Stewart believed that the greater weight and the associated difficulty in handling the ingots would discourage the bandits from escaping with them.

The next day, Stewart's informant told him that Vasquez and his bandits planned to raid the mine on the following morning, load all of the silver they could carry onto two pack mules, and flee to San Francisco, where they could sell it at a good price.

On the morning of the anticipated raid, Stewart left the two large ingots in the building where they had been formed and, taking a pair of binoculars, retreated up the slope of a nearby hill, where he concealed himself behind some brush and waited for the bandits to arrive. Earlier, he had sent his workers away.

About two hours past sunrise, two men on horseback rode up to the headquarters, each leading a mule. Peering through his binoculars, Stewart recognized the newcomers as two men he had beaten at cards several weeks earlier and who were known to be associated with the Vasquez gang from time to time. Finding no one at the headquarters, the two men casually explored the buildings until they discovered the two 500-pound ingots. Amid loud cursing at their mixed luck, they wandered about the premises, gradually acquiring materials from which they constructed a crude tripod with a pulley and sling. With great difficulty, they dragged one of the ingots from the building to the sling and eventually secured it. As they raised the heavy object from the ground, one leg of the tripod snapped, and the entire structure toppled over. Another half-hour of labor resulted in a new tripod that, on the second raising of the heavy ingot, broke and crumpled to the ground.

On the third attempt, the ingot was finally raised and one of the mules led under it. While attempting to lower the ingot into a crate the bandits had strapped to the mule's back, the rope broke. The heavy weight of the falling ingot struck the mule. The startled animal bolted and fled up the hillside, passing within a few feet of Stewart.

By mid-afternoon, as Stewart was tiring of watching the clumsy attempts of the would-be robbers, the two men simply gave up and rode away from the mine, leaving the two ingots lying on the ground. Stewart returned to the headquarters from his hiding place and, convinced that Vasquez would not initiate another attempt at raiding the mine, made preparations to transport the ingots to Los Angeles the following day.

To transport the ingots, Stewart contracted Remi

Nadeau, a freighter who owned a fleet of wagons and a stock of splendid draft animals. Nadeau had the reputation of operating an efficient freight-hauling business and employed several well-armed guards to accompany important shipments. Further, the bandit Vasquez was never known to have robbed a Nadeau shipment.

Stewart was unaware of the reason Vasquez left Nadeau freight wagons alone. Years later, it was learned that Nadeau, while hauling freight one day, came upon a wounded and nearly dead Vasquez along the trail. An hour earlier, Vasquez and his gang had attempted to rob a train. The robbery had failed, the outlaw leader had been badly wounded, and his men had scattered. Nadeau loaded the semi-conscious Vasquez, who had lost a lot of blood, into his wagon, carried him to the freight station, and nursed him back to health. Since that time, a Nadeau-owned freight wagon had never been attacked by Vasquez; at least, not until the day Stewart shipped his large silver ingots.

After the two ingots were loaded into the back of a sturdy wagon, the driver, a man named James Funk, who was accompanied by four armed guards, hauled them to the town of Panamint, where they were transferred to a larger wagon carrying other freight to Los Angeles.

Approaching the city from the south, the freight wagon wound along the twisting trail that snaked through an area today known as Vasquez Rocks. This region is characterized by hundreds of huge granite boulders spread out across more than 1,000 acres. Several of these boulders are in excess of 200 feet tall, are highly weathered, and contain shallow pits eroded out of parts of this igneous, intrusive mass during the past several million years of exposure to the elements. These pits are called tinajas by the Mexicans. Several of these tinajas are three to four feet deep and often support pools of rainwater. Vasquez Rocks often served as a hideout for Tiburcio Vasquez and his gang.

When Funk had driven the freight wagon about halfway through this maze of jumbled boulders, the Vasquez gang attacked. The guards, taken by surprise, surrendered immediately to the fierce-looking band of outlaws. While Funk and the guards were held at gunpoint, Vasquez himself appeared driving a large, sturdy wagon from behind one of the large rocks. After stopping near the freight wagon, Vasquez enlisted the help of two of his compatriots and slid one of the silver ingots onto his wagon. The second ingot was left on Nadeau's wagon.

While the bandits detained Funk and the guards, Vasquez drove his wagon away to some unknown destination in the hills. Twenty minutes later, the bandits sent Funk and company on their way, telling them not to stop until they reached Los Angeles.

On arriving in Los Angeles, Funk reported the robbery to the sheriff. Within minutes, the sheriff had organized a posse and set out for the Vasquez Hills, intent on apprehending the bandits and retrieving Stewart's ingot. Arriving early the following day, the lawmen found Vasquez's wagon within 200 yards of the site of the robbery. The stolen silver ingot was nowhere to be seen. Continued searching yielded no results.

One month later, Tiburcio Vasquez and his gang struck again. The outlaw orchestrated the extortion of $800 from an elderly man named Caralambo, who owned a large ranch near the Los Angeles city limits. (At least one account gives the name of the rancher as Repetto.) As soon as Vasquez departed the Caralambo ranch, the sheriff was alerted and a posse gave chase once again. The lawmen eventually caught up with the bandits near what is now Hollywood. Following a brief shootout, Vasquez, suffering several wounds, was captured and taken to San Jose, where he was charged with a number of offenses. He was made to stand trial a short time later and was found guilty of the murder of two passengers during a previous stagecoach holdup. Vasquez was sentenced to hang.

Several days later, Nadeau arrived at the San Jose jail to visit Vasquez. When he asked the Mexican why, after all the years of leaving the Nadeau freight wagons alone, he had decided to steal the silver ingot, Vasquez replied that he had needed the money badly but reminded Nadeau that he had taken only one of the silver bars.

When Nadeau asked Vasquez what he had done with the ingot he had stolen, the bandit replied that he and his men had dropped it into one of the tinajas in the rocks, not far from where he had taken it from the freight wagon. A few days later, March 19, 1875, Vasquez was hanged. He was 39 years old.

On several occasions during the next few months, both Stewart and Nadeau searched the Vasquez Hills for the 500-pound silver ingot. It was never found. Both men were surprised to discover that there were hundreds of tinajas in the general area of the robbery.

As far as is known, the 500-pound silver ingot has never been found. Searchers for this treasure come and go in the Vasquez Hills, each intent on discovering the hiding place. It has been observed that a number of these tinajas have been partially filled-in with sediment – sand and dust blown into and settled in the area – perhaps effectively burying the ingot.

Today, the actual site of the robbery is in dispute. If the actual location could be discerned, it is logical to assume that the huge bar of silver could be located in one of the tinajas located within 200 yards of that point.

Chapter 9

The Lost Gold Caches of Outlaw Richard Barter

Tiburcio Vasquez was not the only California outlaw known to have cached a treasure. Another was Richard Barter. Though lacking the notoriety of other, more colorful Golden State bad men, Barter proved to be an effective robber, amassing nearly $1 million in gold, currency, and coins over time. Most of his fortune is believed to be buried near the town of Folsom, California, though a second cache of $50,000 was buried in a remote canyon of Trinity Mountain, in Shasta County. To this day, none of Barter's caches have been located.

Richard Barter was born in Canada, the son of a British military officer. As a young man, he heard stories of gold strikes in California and dreamed of traveling to that far western state to make his fortune. When his father passed away a short time later, Barter, along with four relatives, moved to California. They eventually drifted into the Sierra Nevada Range in Placer County and settled in a canyon cut by the North Fork of the American River. Because several placer miners had filed claims nearby, Barter and his party decided to try their luck panning for gold farther up in the glacially fed stream.

For the next several months, the members of the group worked hard but panned only enough gold to barely keep them fed. One by one they drifted away, leaving only Barter to work the small claim.

For supplies, Barter would occasionally travel to the nearby settlement of Auburn. While there, he would spend a couple of days drinking with acquaintances in a tavern. Most of Auburn's citizens admired the young man for sticking to his poor claim, and they perceived him as a hard worker and congenial fellow.

As Barter was leading his supply-laden burro out of Auburn one day in 1853, a group of lawmen led by Deputy Sheriff John Boggs surrounded him and placed him under arrest. As Barter was being escorted to the jail, Boggs informed him that the owner of the town's mercantile had charged him with stealing some merchandise. When word of the arrest got around town, several of Barter's friends raised some money for bail. They also obtained a lawyer for him and the charge was eventually dropped.

Approximately three months later, Barter was arrested again as he rode into Auburn, this time on a charge of stealing a mule. He was tried, found guilty, and sentenced to two years in prison. Just as he was being led from the jail to the carriage waiting to transport him to the penitentiary, however, the real mule thief confessed to the crime. Though

Barter was released, many of the area residents began to regard him as a thief. Soon, placer miners in the area of Barter's camp were accusing him of encroaching on their claims. Shots were occasionally fired into Barter's camp at night and the young man decided it was time to move elsewhere.

Barter made his way to the town of Redding, in Shasta County, about 150 miles to the north. Here, he worked odd jobs to support himself. One day, an Auburn businessman arrived in Redding, recognized Barter, and spread the story that he was a thief. After that, Barter found it difficult to find work. Ironically, he decided to turn to crime to make a living.

For the next several months, Barter robbed lone travelers along the remote roads and trails in Shasta County. When he tired of this, he would raid small placer camps and take whatever gold he could find. Stealing money from unarmed travelers and miners was easy and proved to be lucrative. In time, Barter accumulated a sizeable fortune in gold, currency, and coins. It grew to the degree that the young outlaw stuffed it into saddlebags and transported it on a pack mule. His wanderings eventually took Barter back to Auburn, and for several more months he waylaid travelers and peddlers along the road that ran from that town to Folsom, 20 miles to the south. Following each robbery, Barter would retreat to an old, abandoned, ramshackle cabin that he moved into just outside of Folsom. Here, he buried his loot, each time keeping out only a small amount for himself.

Barter's success and subsequent reputation began to attract other outlaws, and soon he was leading a gang of five or six men. Together, they began terrorizing citizens, farmers, and businessmen throughout Placer County. After each successful robbery, Barter paid off his men and placed his

quick trial, found guilty, and sentenced to life in prison, where he died of consumption a short time later.

While awaiting trial, Barter escaped from the county jail and fled to San Francisco, where he remained hidden for several months. Two years later, he formed a new gang and returned to the business of robbing travelers along the Nevada City–Auburn–Folsom Road. After each robbery, Barter continued to place his share of the loot into his growing hoard near his cabin.

Late one afternoon, Barter and a companion, having just robbed a family of several thousand dollars near Auburn, were returning to Folsom along a seldom-used trail. Unknown to the outlaws, Boggs had learned of the robbery, formed a posse, and set out in pursuit. Riding up on the bandits from behind, Boggs called out for them to surrender. In response, Barter raised a revolver and fired at the lawman. A brief gunfight ensued and Barter was shot twice in the chest, killed instantly. His companion was sentenced to life in prison, where he died a short time later.

No one was left alive who knew the location of the Trinity Mountain cache. In addition to that $50,000, it is estimated that Barter had cached at least another $200,000 in gold, currency, and coin at a secret location in the yard of his old cabin near Folsom. These treasures, likely worth millions today, remain lost.

Chapter 10

W. O. Wilson and the
Happy Bend Treasure

Happy Bend is a tiny community located in Conway County, near the center of the state of Arkansas. Little is left of this century-and-a-half-old settlement save for a few residences, some small farms, a church, and a cemetery. Cattle now graze in meadows where investors once hoped to establish a prosperous and growing town. Before the Civil War, Happy Bend boasted a small mercantile store, a blacksmith shop, and the Wilson Hotel, but something horrible occurred here that soured people from moving into the community. Soon residents moved elsewhere, and the town began to wither away. The story of the demise of Happy Bend involves the bloodthirsty outlaw W. O. Wilson and a buried treasure.

Lewisburg, Arkansas, sits on a bank of the Arkansas River, 10 miles south of Happy Bend. Prior to the Civil War,

Lewisburg was a bustling and prosperous commercial center and served for a time as the seat of governance for Conway County. Steamboats plying up and down the river stopped at Lewisburg to load and unload freight. The town was often boisterous and rowdy, especially when visited by the horse thieves who ranged throughout the Fourche Mountain region to the south. Saloons and gambling houses lined the streets of early Lewisburg, and robbery and murder were commonplace.

Into this setting rode W. O. Wilson. No one ever knew what the initials stood for; all that was known was that he had been born and reared in Alabama and was then run out of his community for stealing from a merchant. For years, Wilson traveled throughout Missouri, Kansas, and Indian Territory. He brought with him a reputation as a horse thief and murderer who loved to brawl, often challenging two men at a time to fight him barehanded. Though he had been arrested for murder on several occasions, he had never been brought to trial.

Wilson was an intimidating figure. He was large and stocky, sporting thick muscular arms, shoulders, and chest. He had bushy eyebrows that met above his nose and he wore a full beard that made his head look bigger than it was. He always wore a black derby hat and a black coat with tails.

Not long after his arrival in Lewisburg, Wilson purchased a parcel of land at Happy Bend, a location on a route well-traveled by those going from Little Rock to Fort Smith by land. On his property he built a two-story, eight-room hotel. He planted flowers around the hotel and procured a black slave woman to do the cooking and cleaning. In a very short time the inn gained a favorable reputation. In spite of his threatening appearance, Wilson was always a charming host, often sitting and conversing with his guests well into the evening.

Soon after the first year of the inn's operation, strange stories began to circulate about travelers checking in and never being seen or heard from again. When confronted by his neighbors about these suspicions, Wilson always remained pleasant and invited an inspection of his property. Nothing was ever found to suggest wrongdoing.

Wilson continued to prosper over the next few years. He succeeded, in fact, far and above the degree one might expect from a small-town hotel operator. Now and then a new story would surface concerning the mysterious disappearance of a visitor to the inn. On several occasions, the law was called out to investigate, but nothing ever came of the visits.

One day an influential rancher and businessman from Galla Rock, Arkansas, named Paschal checked into the hotel and vanished. Once again lawmen were called in. While searching the grounds, a deputy was informed by two young boys that they had found a dead horse in a thicket not far from the inn. The deputy identified the dead horse as belonging to Paschal. It had been tied to a tree far from graze and had evidently starved to death. The lawmen were convinced that Wilson had hidden the horse in the thicket intending to return for it, but his neighbors' constant surveillance kept him from carrying out the plan. Wilson and the slave woman were arrested and taken to Lewisburg, where they were bound and guarded on the second floor of a store. The woman refused to answer any questions from the authorities and cast fearful glances at Wilson. Her behavior left the impression that she was more terrified of Wilson than of her interrogators.

On the following evening, Wilson managed to escape from his second-floor confinement and slip down to the riverbank. There, he stole a skiff, pushed out into the water, and fled downstream. Pursuers, who arrived at the shore just as he was entering the river, opened fire, and another group of men launched a boat in an effort to catch the fugitive. When they caught up with Wilson, they found him lying in the bottom of the skiff, bleeding to death from the wounds inflicted by the riflemen.

The next morning, on hearing of the death of her master, the slave woman expressed visible relief. When she calmed down, she related a most amazing story. She revealed the existence of a cleverly concealed trapdoor in the floor of one of the ground-level guest rooms of the hotel that led to a deep underground cellar. Searchers had failed to discover the trapdoor during their earlier visits. The slave woman stated that Wilson would club an unsuspecting guest on the head with a heavy mallet and carry the limp form to the cellar. There, the victim would be stripped of all valuables – coins, watches, jewelry, spurs, and even gold teeth – which Wilson would place in a flour sack. He would knot the sack and have the woman hold it while he turned his attention to the victim. To the woman's absolute horror, Wilson would hack the body into small pieces with a meat cleaver. Then he would force the woman to place the dismembered pieces into weighted sacks and, as he accompanied her, would order her to drag them over to Point Remove Creek, one mile to the north – a task that required at least three trips. Here, the sacks would be tossed into the swirling waters of the stream, to disappear forever into the soft bottom. This done, Wilson would send the woman back to the hotel. The slave woman told her interrogators that she believed that once she was out of sight, Wilson would bury the sack of valuables. He would return to the hotel 30 minutes later.

She estimated that he had buried several dozen sacks over the three years she had been with him.

When the news of Wilson's grisly activities reached the residents of Happy Bend, they were so horrified and repulsed that they set fire to the inn and burned it to the ground, determined to remove it from their sight forever.

Law officers searched long and hard for the place where Wilson buried his stolen goods, but they were never able to find anything. Today, treasure hunters armed with sophisticated electronic detecting equipment come to the area but have had little luck. A few coins and a spur have been recovered near the creek, but nothing else substantial has ever been reported found.

Since Wilson's Hotel was destroyed well over a century ago, no one in Happy Bend today is certain of the original location. It is known, however, that the place where the bodies were dumped into the west fork of Point Remove Creek was at a point just north of the Happy Bend settlement and a little to the northwest of Goose Pond. This is the exact location where the treasure hunters found the coins and spur.

Today Happy Bend is a small, quiet community of approximately 20 families. Interstate 40 passes some 10 miles to the south, but there are no direct exits off that busy highway to the tiny village; thus it remains relatively secluded and isolated. Hunters flock to the area during deer season, but otherwise very few people have reason to travel the dirt roads to this locale. Now and then a resident of Happy Bend will encounter a treasure hunter swinging a metal detector back and forth along the banks of Point Remove Creek or around Goose Pond.

Recent studies of Point Remove Creek suggest that the continued searches for W. O. Wilson's buried treasure may be

members to lawmen's bullets. Parrott compensated for this by pocketing the dead men's share of the most recent robbery loot.

Parrott and his followers eventually found that their ability to travel freely in Wyoming was becoming limited. He decided to take his gang to Montana, where outlaws continued to rob gold shipments from stagecoaches. When Parrott learned that some area mercantile establishments purchased gold ore from the miners, he robbed these too. After several successful heists, the gang returned to Wyoming, their horses bearing heavy loads of gold. Parrott again buried his share at his North Butte cache.

Parrott and his gang decided to rob a train carrying a large payroll to the mining town of Carbon. At a location between Laramie and Medicine Bow, they pried the spikes from the rails and lay in wait for the train. However, an alert section hand noticed something was amiss and notified authorities, who stopped all trains.

Two law enforcement officers – Wyoming Deputy Sheriff Robert Widdowfield and Union Pacific Detective Tip Vincent – went to investigate. Parrott grew suspicious, however, when train traffic stopped. He decided to leave and led his companions away toward Elk Mountain. The lawmen gave chase, closing in from behind.

Hours later, Widdowfield and Vincent stopped to examine an abandoned campfire along the trail. A moment later, shots rang out from hiding and the two were killed. Later, a member of the gang, Dutch Charlie Bates (also known as Burris), was captured and transported to Rawlins to await trail. During the trip to Rawlins, Bates confessed everything to lawmen. He identified Parrott as the leader of the gang and the mastermind behind the robberies. He also told them that Parrott took his share of the robbery loot and buried it in a secret location near North Butte.

When the train stopped for fuel and water at Carbon, an angry mob stormed the railroad car transporting Bates. They dragged him from the car and hanged him from a nearby telegraph pole.

After learning of Bates's fate, Parrott decided to lie low for a time, hoping the lawmen would eventually forget about him. For months, he hid among the Missouri River Breaks of eastern Montana.

Accounts of what followed vary. One has Parrott and his remaining accomplice riding to Helena, Montana. In spite of the fact that wanted posters with Parrott's likeness were tacked up on trees, telegraph poles, and storefronts every few feet and that his odd facial feature made him quite recogniz-able, the outlaws decided to enter the Last Chance Gulch Sa-loon for a drink. Within minutes, Parrott was surrounded by three lawmen, each holding a gun to his head. Parrott was arrested, cuffed, and shackled.

A second account has Parrott and his fellow outlaw ar-rested in Miles City after boasting of killing the two lawmen who followed them after the aborted train robbery. Whichever account is true, one thing that is known for certain is that Parrott was placed on a train bound for Rawlins.

Following a trial, Parrott was found guilty of murder and sentenced to hang on April 2, 1881. While waiting in jail, Par-rott learned that a number of Rawlins citizens were planning to take him from the jail and hang him. Using a pocketknife and a piece of sandstone, Parrott was able to weaken the riv-ets on the shackles around his ankles. On March 22, he re-moved the restraints and hid in a washroom. Later, when jailor Robert Rankin arrived in the area, Parrott, swinging the shackles, struck him over the head, fracturing his skull. Rankin was still able to fight back, and as he did so, he called for his wife, who entered the room with a revolver, forcing Parrott back into his cell.

The attempted escape was the tipping point. When the townsfolk learned of this, they gathered in a mob estimated to number close to 200 people, burst into the jail and, while holding a gun on Rankin, dragged Parrott from his cell. Once outside, they hauled him to a telegraph pole and hanged him.

The following morning, John E. Osborne, a Rawlins physician, took possession of Parrott's body. He had it carried to his office, where it was laid on an operating table. Osborne performed a cursory autopsy and then sawed off the top of Parrott's skull to examine the outlaw's brain for abnormalities. Later, he cleaned out the skullcap and used it as an ashtray for his cigars.

As if this were not unusual enough, Osborne carefully removed the skin from Parrott's body, had it tanned, and commissioned a local shoemaker to fashion a pair of shoes and a medical bag with it. The doctor gave the remaining pieces of the skin to friends. Dr. Osborne was later elected governor of Wyoming. It is written that during his inauguration, he wore the shoes he'd had made from the skin of Big Nose George Parrott.

Osborne eventually presented the top half of Parrott's skull to Lillian Heath, who had assisted him during the autopsy. Heath went on to become Wyoming's first female physician. Parrott's skullcap was used as a doorstop in her medical office.

Authorities determined that Parrott's remains should not desecrate the town's cemetery. The body was placed in a discarded whiskey barrel and buried in an unknown location.

During the 1950s, workmen digging in an alley in Rawlins encountered an old whiskey barrel. Inside were human bones and a skull that was missing its top. When Parrott's skullcap was obtained from Dr. Heath's possessions, it perfectly matched the partial skull that had been unearthed.

With the death of Big Nose George Parrott, no one was left alive who knew the location of his buried loot in the Pumpkin Buttes region. Because so little was known of Parrott and his cache until recent years, there have been very few attempts to locate the site of his treasure. As far as is known, Parrott's wealth, which at today's values would be substantial, has never been found. A conservative estimate of the gold, jewelry, coins, and currency he buried from livestock rustling and stagecoach robberies is $150,000. If found today, the cache would be worth well over $1 million.

Chapter 12

The Lost Jesse James Cache

Jesse James is arguably one of the most notorious and well-known outlaws ever to grace the American historical landscape. His criminal escapades, many of them exaggerated, have found their way into biographies, novels, and films. It is true that the James Gang robbed trains, banks, and stagecoaches and in the process made off with a considerable amount of wealth in the form of gold, coins, and currency. Many of these robberies have been documented; others are conjecture. For a time, any robbery committed in or near Arkansas, Kansas, or Missouri was attributed to the James Gang, whether that was true or not.

Jesse James and his gang hailed from Missouri but were well-known as far away as Texas, Kentucky, and Tennessee. They were known to ride with the Younger Gang on occasion.

They often hid out in Arkansas and frequently visited the town of Little Rock.

During one of their trips to Arkansas, Jesse and his gang robbed a stagecoach at a location in the Ouachita Mountains between the towns of Hot Springs and Malvern. At the time, the identity of the robbers was unknown, though the James Gang was suspected. In his later years, Frank James admitted that it was he and brother Jesse, along with several members of their gang, that were involved. Frank claimed that it was his idea to rob the stage and that he planned and executed the heist to perfection. According to researchers, the gang consisted of Jesse and Frank James, along with Cole, John, and Bob Younger, and possibly Clell Miller.

On January 5, 1874, the Hot Springs–Malvern stage-coach run was traversing a somewhat remote portion of the Ouachita Mountains. The stage, pulled by six stout horses, carried mail and a contingent of passengers. At one point along the road the driver spotted several men up ahead, and when he got closer, he saw that they were dressed as Union soldiers – a disguise the James Gang affected from time to time. The strangers had little difficulty in convincing the driver to stop the stage. By the time the driver realized his mistake, it was too late.

After the coach was stopped, the driver was held at gun-point and the passengers were ordered out of the vehicle. Cole Younger asked the passengers if any of them had fought for the Confederacy. One man, G. R. Crump, stepped forward and admitted that he had. Younger stated that they only robbed from Unionists, not from those who fought for or sup-ported the Confederacy. Crump was allowed to keep his money and possessions, while the others were robbed of their money, jewelry, and watches. From the coach, the outlaws took the mail pouches and an express package. During those days, money was often sent via the post, and the outlaws knew it. Before sending the stagecoach on its way, Jesse took two of the six horses pulling the coach.

The robbery went off smoothly, save for the arrival of a posse of lawmen. Shortly after the coach pulled away, agents of law enforcement were spotted in the distance and headed toward the outlaws. The lawmen were on another mission, but when informed of the robbery by the stagecoach driver, they hastened toward the scene of the crime.

At the robbery site, the outlaws examined the take and counted the money. Some estimates have the total take at less than $2,000, while some evidence indicates that the robbery netted as much as $32,000. (A short time after the robbery, a newspaper article appeared stating that the mail pouches were carrying $32,000 in cash.) While the outlaws were thus occupied, one of them glanced up and spotted the oncoming lawmen. Jesse and Frank decided that hiding the stolen loot offered the best chance to get away. If caught, they reasoned, it would not be among their possessions and they would likely be released. In haste, the outlaws excavated a shallow hole not far from the road they were traveling. They dumped the loot into this hole and refilled it. Atop the hole, Frank James place a large, flat stone upon which he and Jesse scratched their names as well as some cryptic figures. The outlaws mounted up and rode away, intending to return at some future date and retrieve the stolen goods. According to Frank James during a later interview, the outlaws were never able to return to the site. For years, the flat stone marker lay undisturbed atop the buried fortune.

In 1928, an area famer named Gilpin was on an errand that took him down what the old-timers still referred to as the Hot Springs–Malvern Stagecoach Road. At one point along the road, he pulled his horse-drawn wagon to a halt, climbed down, and relieved himself. As he turned and prepared to climb back into the wagon, he spotted a large, flat slab of sandstone with some marks chiseled on it. On closer inspection, Gilpin discerned the names "Frank and Jesse James" along with the figure "$32,000." In addition to the letters and numbers, the rock bore the figures of a cross, a Bowie knife, and a three-pronged fork.

Gilpin had no idea what any of this meant, but the notion of possessing a stone that bore the names of the famous James brothers appealed to him. He removed the stone from its position and placed it in the back of his wagon. When he returned home that evening, he showed the stone to his wife and then leaned it against a tree in the front yard. Over the years, he took great delight in pointing it out to visitors.

With the passage of time, the novelty of the stone wore off and Gilpin placed it in a shed. Several months later, a friend stopped by to borrow a tool and spotted the stone. He asked Gilpin about it and the farmer explained how he found it along the old stagecoach road. The visitor told Gilpin that such stones were often used to mark a location where treasure was buried.

It wasn't long after that when Gilpin received another visitor. On seeing the stone with the markings scratched onto it, the visitor wondered aloud if it had anything to do with the James Gang's robbery of a stagecoach in the vicinity many years earlier. The visitor told Gilpin about the outlaws robbing a coach and taking money and jewelry from the passengers.

Though several years had passed since he found the flat rock, Gilpin decided he would return to the area and try to relocate the exact spot, dig into the ground and retrieve the treasure. When he arrived at what he thought was the correct location, he became confused and disoriented. In the years since he had last visited the area, it had changed dramatically. Logging had disturbed some of the forest cover. A recent forest fire had further changed the appearance of the environment, and floods that had occurred over the years had modified much of the landscape. Gilpin dug several holes over a wide area but by the end of the day, he had found nothing. Discouraged, he returned home.

Over the next several years, Gilpin returned to the approximate area where he had first found the stone. In all, as he told friends, he must have dug a thousand holes in search of the buried treasure.

As far as anyone can tell, the treasure cache is still there, in the exact same place where it was buried by Jesse and Frank James and their gang in 1874. With the passage of nearly a century and a half, the contents of the cache are worth far more than they were originally. Collector values alone relating to the currency and the jewelry and watches would make the cache a truly rich find.

The route of last century's Hot Springs–Malvern Stagecoach route can still be found on old maps. With some diligence and persistence, the location of the robbery could likely be determined within a few dozen feet. With the proper equipment, it is possible that some fortunate treasure hunter may find it.

Chapter 13

Pirate Jean Lafitte's
Galveston Island Treasure

Outlaws come in all shapes and sizes and practice their trade in a variety of settings. When we think of outlaws, we generally conjure images of ne'er-do-wells holding up banks, trains, and stagecoaches and making off with loot, occasionally shooting someone in the process. Some of the most effective outlaws associated with North American history, however, plied their trade not on land but at sea. We know them by their popular name: pirates.

One of the most colorful and successful pirates was Jean Lafitte. Most Lafitte biographers claim he was born in France, but the truth is, no one knows for certain. Lafitte himself once claimed that he he had born in Bordeaux, France, in 1780. His parents, he said, were Sephardic Jews who had fled Spain for France during the 1760s. On another occasion, Lafitte stated that he had been born in the French city of Bayonne. Other of Lafitte's claimed birthplaces have included Brest and Saint-Malo. One of Lafitte's biographers suggests that it was convenient for the pirate to claim France as a birthplace because it provided him some element of protection from American law. Other accounts list Lafitte's origins as Orduna, Spain, and Westchester, New York. Author Jack C. Ramsey has introduced the notion that Lafitte was born in Haiti. (Although it is believed the pirate's name was originally spelled "Laffite," most published documents found in the United States render the name as "Lafitte." As that remains the most common usage, that is the name that will be employed here.)

Regardless of where he was from, Lafitte, as a young man, was living in America. He was fascinated with the bayou country of Louisiana and spent days exploring as much of it as possible. In time, this interest led to the exploration of inlets, harbors, and other locations eastward along the Mississippi coast and westward along the coast of Texas. While Jean was learning much about the geography of the Gulf Coast, his older brother Pierre was operating as a privateer out of Saint-Domingue. Evidence suggests that Pierre brought captured merchandise to New Orleans to sell and that he was assisted in this endeavor by his brother Jean.

By 1812, Jean Lafitte had grown tired of his role as a broker of stolen cargo. He saw some advantage in capturing the cargo himself and eliminating the middleman. With that in mind, he and Pierre purchased a schooner and employed a man named Trey Cook to captain it. As the schooner did not apply for a commission from the government, it was operating illegally. According to the law, such a vessel was regarded as a pirate ship.

In January 1813, the Lafitte brothers captured a Spanish slave ship. They later sold the slaves, along with some of the additional cargo, and pocketed $18,000. The brothers converted the slave ship into a pirate vessel and named it the Dorada. After capturing another ship using the Dorada, the Lafitte brothers deemed it a less-than-useful pirate vessel and returned it to its owners. As a pirate, Lafitte gained a reputation as a gentleman. He always treated captured crewmen well and freed them at the first opportunity. Captured goods were taken back to New Orleans and sold.

Acting governor of Louisiana Thomas B. Robertson was perturbed by the piracy activities of the Lafitte brothers. While the residents of the Louisiana coast appreciated the Lafittes for providing them with goods at a low cost, Robertson referred to them as "brigands who infest our coast and overrun our country." When Governor William C. C. Claiborne returned to office and sent Robertson back to his previous duties, he relaxed the official pressure on the Lafittes.

On June 18, 1812, the United States declared war on Great Britain, despite being at a naval disadvantage. While Great Britain had a powerful navy, the U. S. had only a few ships. In order to fortify the navy, the U. S. government offered letters of marque to private vessels. A letter of marque authorized a private citizen – a privateer – to attack and capture enemy vessels and bring them before admiralty courts for possession and sale. One such letter was granted to Jean Lafitte. While Lafitte turned over some small amount of the captured booty to the authorities, most of it was sold illegally through his and Pierre's operation. When this became clear to the authorities and they realized how much revenue they were losing from Lafitte's illegal activities, they set out to prevent him from continuing this practice.

On November 10, 1812, U. S. District Attorney John R. Grimes filed charges against Lafitte for "violation of revenue law." Three days later, Jean and Pierre Lafitte were captured, along with 25 of their crewmen. Contraband was confiscated but while the authorities were distracted, the Lafittes escaped.

In March 1813, Jean Lafitte registered as the captain of a brig. While he listed his job as piloting the vessel on a trip to New York, he was, in truth, establishing himself as a privateer. Not long afterward, he obtained a letter of marque from the country of Columbia. Although he captured ships and seized cargo, he never returned any of it to Cartagena in northern Columbia, directing it instead to the port of New Orleans, where he and Pierre continued to sell it.

This blatant disregard for his laws angered Governor Claiborne, who began making plans to capture the bandits. He appointed his revenue officers to prepare an ambush. In addition, a $500 reward was offered for the capture of Jean Lafitte. In return, Lafitte had dozens of handbills printed up to hand out and tack up on walls that offered a $500 reward for the governor.

In January 1814, Lafitte arranged the auction of a large amount of contraband outside of New Orleans. Federal authorities attempted to break up the operation, and in the process, one of the revenue officers was killed and two others wounded. In addition to these difficulties, New Orleans merchants were putting pressure on the governor to do something about Lafitte because the pirate was charging lower prices for the same goods. Claiborne responded to the ongoing difficulties by approaching the state legislature and requesting approval to establish a militia company to remove the pirates from Louisiana once and for all. The legislature appointed a committee to study the matter, but the truth was they were in no hurry to roust Lafitte, as many of their constituents benefitted from the pirates' sales of goods. A short time later, Pierre Lafitte was arrested, convicted, and jailed on charges related to acts of piracy.

The jailing and conviction of Pierre did not deter Jean one whit. While his brother was incarcerated, Jean operated the piracy and smuggling business with impunity. In response to Lafitte, as well as other pirates, the British Navy increased patrols throughout the Gulf of Mexico. In August 1814, they established a naval base at Pensacola. In September, a British ship fired on one of Lafitte's vessels and gave pursuit. Lafitte took to shallow water, where the larger British ship could not follow. The British commander raised a white flag and indicated that he wanted to talk. He had a dinghy lowered into the water. Moments later, several officers climbed into the boat, took seats, and were all rowed toward Lafitte's ship. Lafitte likewise lowered a rowboat and went out to meet them halfway.

The captain of the British ship, Nicholas Lockyer, along with Royal Marine Infantry Captain John McWiliams, had been transporting a package, with orders to deliver it to Lafitte. Lafitte invited the men to row to the nearby island. On arriving, the officers were surrounded by Lafitte's men as the pirate identified himself to them. The officers handed over the package.

Inside was a letter from King George III, who offered Lafitte and his pirates full British citizenship, as well as land grants in the British colonies in the Americas, if they promised to assist in the naval fight against the United States. The letter stated that if Lafitte refused, they would bombard Barataria, a known pirate haven south of New Orleans and a base of operations for the pirate. The second letter was from Lieutenant Colonel Edward Nicholls of the Royal Marines, urging the pirate to accept the offer.

Lafitte realized that, regarding his operation in Barataria Bay, he would eventually have to fight either the U. S. or the British. He felt that he had a better chance of defeating the U. S. forces, so he decided to align with them. Lafitte sent a message to U. S. officials, informing them that some of his men wanted to side with the British, but that they would align with the American forces on the condition that Pierre be released. The offer was accepted.

On September 13, 1814, U. S. Navy Commodore Daniel Patterson led a warship, six gunboats, and a tender into Barataria Bay and began shelling ships and the settlements on the shore. Ten of the pirate ships formed a battle line in the bay and returned fire, but it became clear that the U. S. forces were winning. Lafitte, realizing the outcome of the battle, ordered his men to abandon the ships. Several of the vessels were set afire. When Patterson's troopers arrived on the shore, they met no resistance, took 80 captives and captured eight pirate ships and $500,000 worth of stolen goods, but could not locate Lafitte, who had escaped into the nearby forests and swamps.

Governor Claiborne wrote letters to U. S. Attorney General Richard Rush and General Andrew Jackson. Claiborne requested a pardon for the Baratarians and implied that Commodore Patterson had erred in destroying the "first line of defense for Louisiana."

In mid-December 1814, Andrew Jackson arrived in New Orleans and met with Jean Lafitte. Lafitte offered to help defend New Orleans against the British if the United States would pardon any of his men who agreed to join in the fight.

Jackson agreed to the terms, and on December 19, the state legislature recommended a full pardon. Encouraged by Lafitte, many of his men joined the New Orleans militia or volunteered to serve as sailors on the ships. The rest formed three artillery companies.

On December 23, several ships of the British fleet sailed up the Mississippi River toward New Orleans. Lafitte noted that the American line of defense did not extend far enough to keep the British from encircling the American troops. Lafitte told Jackson that it was necessary to extend the line into the swamps, and Jackson gave the order to do so. The British commenced firing on the Americans on December 28 but were driven off by an artillery company manned by two of Lafitte's former lieutenants.

During the ensuing battles, Lafitte's men distinguished themselves in helping defeat the British. Even Jackson voiced praise for the bravery and skill of the former pirates. With Jackson's recommendation, the U. S. government granted full pardons to Jean and Pierre Lafitte as well as all of the men who had served under them. The pardons were granted on February 6, 1815.

In January 1816, Jean and Pierre Lafitte made an agreement with Spain to serve as spies. At the time, Spain was involved in a war with Mexico, which was fighting for independence. Jean was ordered to Galveston, on the Texas Gulf Coast. At the time, Texas belonged to Spain. Galveston served as a headquarters for the pirate Louis Michel-Aury, a French privateer who sympathized with the Mexicans' ideals. During March or April 1817, Lafitte assumed command of Galveston Island. Lafitte found the island ideal for his needs: It was essentially uninhabited save for his own men and the Karankawa Indians, and it was outside the authority of the

United States. He lost no time in establishing it as a base for his smuggling operations. Lafitte's crewmen tore down the house constructed by Michel-Aury and built dozens of new ones to house crewmembers and their families.

Before 1817 ended, Lafitte's colony, which he called Campeche, boasted a population of almost 200 men and women. Newcomers to the island were required to sign a loyalty oath to the pirate. Lafitte remained busy attacking and capturing merchant and slave ships. The Galveston Island location served the pirate well until a series of mishaps arose. After some of his men kidnapped a Karankawa woman, the Indians attacked the colony and killed five men. Lafitte's gunboats rained fire on the Karankawa encampment, killing most of its inhabitants. Not long afterward, a hurricane devastated the island; most of the houses were destroyed, along with several ships. Lafitte continued use the island as a base from time to time, but it was never the same. As a result, he often operated out of Matagorda Bay, 100 miles to the southwest.

In 1820, Lafitte reportedly married Madeline Regaud, the daughter of a French colonist. They had a son, Jean Pierre Lafitte. In 1821, the USS Enterprise was ordered to Galveston Island to remove Lafitte and his pirates once and for all in response to the pirate's attack on an American merchant ship. Lafitte met with the captain of the Enterprise, a man named Kearney. After several days of discussions and negotiations between the pirate and Kearny, Lafitte ordered the hanging of two men who he said were responsible for the attack on the American ship, in the hope that this would appease the captain. Kearney was not impressed with Lafitte's gesture. He ordered the guns of the Enterprise aimed toward the island and gave Lafitte 30 days to vacate. Lafitte agreed to depart without a fight.

Several days before the period was to expire, one of Lafitte's ships, the Pride, was somehow forced aground near the mouth of the Lavaca River in Matagorda Bay. A number of hull planks were fractured and the vessel sank. The Pride was known to have been carrying a great quantity of treasure taken during raids of several Spanish ships in the Gulf of Mexico. Lafitte, in the company of several crewmen, sailed to the site and recovered a wooden chest filled with treasure, along with two canvas sacks containing silver ingots. The booty was carried to shore. After dividing much of it among his crew, Lafitte assigned two men to ready the remainder for burial. Lafitte and his sailors hauled the treasure several hundred yards across the salt marsh, selected a suitable location, and buried it.

Lafitte took a compass reading and a bearing on two nearby mottes, or groves of trees – Kentucky Motte and Mauldin Motte. The pirate made some notes in his journal, and when he was finished, he took a long brass rod he had carried from the ship and shoved it deep into the ground just above the treasure until only eight inches remained visible. Lafitte then told his two companions that if they returned to the site after three years and found the treasure still there, they could have it. This done, Lafitte sailed back to Galveston Island.

Before vacating the island, Lafitte and his men burned all of the standing structures and buried most of the stolen cargo. Several of the crewmen were arrested and later convicted of piracy. Those who were not captured joined Lafitte aboard one of his ships. When Lafitte informed them that he was returning to piracy, half of the men refused to accompany him. He allowed them to depart and told them that they could take his other ship, the General Victoria. That night,

Lafitte, apparently in a vengeful mood, led his pirates aboard the General Victoria, where they crippled the ship by destroying the masts and spars. Lafitte sailed away, never to return to Galveston Island.

For the next several months, Lafitte preyed on Spanish ships in the Gulf of Mexico. When he had filled his hold with stolen cargo, he returned to the barrier islands near New Orleans, where he would unload it and replenish his supplies. Brother Pierre handled the sale of the contraband. As this was going on, the congressional delegation of Louisiana petitioned the federal government to do something about Lafitte and put an end to the piracy and smuggling. In response, ships from the U. S. Navy were sent to the Gulf.

During the ensuing weeks, a number of pirates were put out of commission. In November 1821, Lafitte was fired upon, pursued, and captured. On February 13, 1822, he escaped. Once free, Lafitte acquired more ships and established a pirate base on the island of Cuba as a result of bribing local elected officials. In April, as he set his sights on seizing an American merchant ship, he was captured again. The Americans turned him over to the Cuban authorities, who promptly released him.

Lafitte continued to prey on ships in the Caribbean. Unfortunately, several of the ships he captured and pillaged were carrying important and necessary goods to Cuba. This angered Cuban officials, who sought to put an end to Lafitte's depredations. With the increased pressure, Lafitte made an arrangement with Columbia to raid Spanish ships.

On February 4, 1823, Lafitte's ship engaged in a battle with two Spanish merchant vessels. The Spaniards were heavily armed and inflicted great damage to the pirate ship. During the onslaught, Lafitte was severely wounded. According to reports, he died on the morning of February 5 and was buried at sea. Though never verified, other rumors circulated that Lafitte escaped and fled to the Carolinas, where he subsequently lived in anonymity.

Lafitte has been gone a long time, but many believe that the treasures he cached in various locations are yet to be found and recovered. With regard to the Lavaca River treasure, according to legend, one of the trusted companions who helped him cache it died from malaria within a few months of Lafitte's departure from the island. Before he died, however, he related an account of the burial to a friend. Using the directions provided by the late pirate, the friend made several unsuccessful trips to locate the chest and the silver ingots.

The second pirate who assisted with the burial of the treasure never returned to the site, choosing instead to remain in New Orleans and raise a family. As an old man, the former buccaneer told the story of the buried chest of gold and jewels to his two sons. With great enthusiasm and certain of their ability to find the treasure, the sons organized an expedition to the Lavaca River marsh, but they, too, failed.

More time passed, and a man named Hill sought to establish a ranch on the land at the junction of the Lavaca River and the Gulf of Mexico stocked the grassy marshes with fine horses and cattle. One of Hill's employees was a black man named Ward, who Hill had placed in charge of the livestock. Ward's responsibilities included running horses and cattle out into the marsh during the day to graze and returning them to the pens each night.

While the livestock were grazing in the marsh during the day, Ward would sometimes lie down on the grassy sward and take a nap. One afternoon, as he was tending the stock on horseback, he grew drowsy and searched for a good spot to stretch out on the soft ground. Dismounting, he looked around for something to which he could tie his horse. Nearby, he found the tip of a brass rod sticking out of the ground. After hitching the horse to the rod, Ward lay down a few paces away and dozed off.

The horse Ward was using on this day was unaccustomed to being staked. He pulled at the rod, bending it and extracting almost its entire length. When Ward awoke from his nap, he pulled the rod completely out if the ground and carried it back with him when he returned with the stock, intending to show it to his employer.

Rancher Hill was familiar with the tale of Jean Lafitte's buried treasure, and when he saw the long brass rod, he knew immediately what it was. Hill told Ward he wanted to be taken the next morning to the place in the marsh where the rod had been found. The two men searched throughout the marsh the following day, but Ward was unable to locate the spot where he had lain down to nap.

In 1870, a man was turkey hunting near the mouth of the Lavaca River. On spotting a flock of birds several dozen yards away, he got down on his hands and knees and crawled toward his quarry. As he was slowly creeping along on all fours, the turkey hunter's knee struck hard against something partially buried in the ground. When he turned to examine what it was that had brought him pain, he saw what he thought was a low pile of small bricks. Wondering why bricks would be in this remote location, he placed one in his pouch, intending to examine it later.

On returning home, the hunter removed the heavy brick from the pouch and showed it to his brother. The brother scratched the surface of the object with his penknife and discovered that it was almost pure silver. Familiar with the story of the hidden treasure cache of pirate Lafitte, the turkey hunter deduced that he had stumbled onto a portion of the lost cache.

When the brothers sought the location of the pile of silver the next day, they could not find it. Though the two men searched several miles of the grassy marsh, the sameness of the region throughout its extent made it difficult to pinpoint any specific location. They searched in the area of Mauldin Motte and Kentucky Motte, but neither man was aware of their relationship to the cache.

Another man may have actually found Lafitte's treasure cache, but it seems likely that he only removed a few gold coins from it. A rather eccentric local resident known as Crazy Ben was known to most in the area but was seldom taken seriously and remained unfriendly to all. The old man was never known to hold down a job, and he lived in squalor in an old shack near the mouth of the Lavaca River. What distinguished Crazy Ben from other area residents was the fact that he paid for his drinks with gold Spanish coins.

Crazy Ben often told the story that, when he had served as a cabin boy to the pirate Jean Lafitte, he had secretly followed the famous buccaneer across the salt marsh and watched as he buried his chests filled with treasure. When the pirates fled the area several days later, Ben, no more than 10 years old at the time, remained on the south bank of Clear Creek, near Galveston Bay, working as a fisherman and handyman and when times were lean he occasionally begged for handouts. After several years had passed and Ben was certain that Lafitte was never going to return to retrieve his buried treasure, he went to the site, dug up the chest, and helped himself to a handful of coins. After pocketing the pieces, he reburied the chest. With the money in his pocket,

Ben was able to live well and drink his fill for several weeks. When he finally ran out of cash, he simply returned to the cache and retrieved more coins.

An unambitious man, Crazy Ben preferred to drift around the bay area, visiting a number of different taverns and spending his coins on ale. During his common alcohol-fuelled conversations with fellow drinkers, Ben would admit to deriving his income from the buried treasure chest of the pirate Jean Lafitte. Word of the source of the old man's wealth spread throughout the region, and from time to time men would attempt to follow him into the marsh. Ben always managed to elude them.

One evening after a full day of drinking at a local tavern, Crazy Ben staggered out of the establishment and down the street toward his shack. Moments later, two shadowy figures left the tavern and followed him into the night. That evening was the last time anyone saw Crazy Ben alive. The following morning, his body was found washed up on the shore of the bay near Clear Creek, not far from his home. His throat had been slashed, and most believed he was killed because he would not reveal the location of the Lafitte treasure.

A number of attempts to locate the treasure cache of Jean Lafitte have been made during the past century and a half. During the 1920s, a man arrived in the area from Oklahoma with what he claimed were the original hand-written notes from Lafitte's journal describing the location of the buried treasure chest. Although the newcomer had no trouble locating the two prominent mottes, he was unable to find the cache.

The search continues.

Chapter 14

Henry Plummer's Lost Gold

A number of western states claim famous and notorious outlaws as part of their colorful history: New Mexico is linked to Billy the Kid, Missouri was the home of Frank and Jesse James, California boasted Tiburcio Vasquez, and Wyoming claims Butch Cassidy and the Sundance Kid. In the annals of Montana history, no single outlaw approaches the notoriety and repute accorded Henry Plummer. The western part of this picturesque and magnificent state is steeped in the legend and lore of this colorful and infamous criminal, and the tales of his buried treasures have lured hundreds of fortune hunters from around the country in search of them. A few of the treasures have been found, but the majority of Plummer's buried loot remains lost, still tempting and attracting the hopeful as it has for over a century.

As notorious as Plummer was, and as much newspaper space as has been devoted to his nefarious activities, his background prior to arriving in the American West is unknown. Many are convinced that he came from somewhere in the east, that he was a man of education and distinction, and it has been written that he often conducted himself as a refined and cultured gentleman. On arriving in the region of the Rocky Mountains, however, Plummer learned quickly that fortunes could be made more easily through robbery and murder than through hard work. He thereafter devoted himself to the business of taking other people's money and gold via unlawful and despicable acts.

Plummer led a varied life during his time in the West. Though known primarily as an outlaw, he was also a successful gambler – and even a lawman. Eventually, however, he came to be known as "The Scourge of the Rockies," and history suggests that he stole more money and gold than any other famous outlaw of the American west.

It is believed that Plummer first landed in Nevada when he came west; at least, that is where his story begins. As a result of his implication in a number of illegal activities there, mostly robbery, he was run out of the state by law enforcement authorities. He fled to California, where he found the pickings much easier, and for the next year, he robbed miners of their hard-earned gold until officials there began making things hot for him. Just barely one step ahead of the law, Plummer fled to the state of Washington, where he set himself up as a gambler.

Plummer became very successful manning a poker table in Walla Walla – so successful, in fact, that many of those who lost suspected him of running a crooked game. Though he was never caught cheating, Plummer closed down his game and moved on to other activities. It was said that he missed the adventure and excitement associated with robbing miners, travelers, and stagecoaches. Some writers have even suggested that Plummer took a perverse joy in being pursued by lawmen and that gambling never held the same thrill for him.

As Plummer was contemplating a return to the gold fields of California, he got into trouble in Walla Walla. Some say a woman was involved, but whatever the reason, he was run out of town. Weeks later he rode into Lewiston, Idaho, and decided to remain for a while.

At Lewiston, Plummer encountered a number of men, all thieves and murderers, who he believed would comprise an efficient and effective gang. Within a short span of time they were aggressively robbing stagecoaches, freight wagons, miners, and travelers, often killing their victims so they would never be able to identify the perpetrators. In a matter of just a few months, the Plummer Gang amassed an impressive fortune in gold ingots, coins, and nuggets. From the first successful robbery, the gang was constantly pursued by lawmen.

One of Plummer's gang members was a man named Jack Cleveland. Cleveland was a constant thorn in Plummer's side but because he was a fearless robber and a ruthless killer, the leader liked having him around. Once, in a fit of drunken rage, Cleveland got into an argument with a fellow gang member over a petty matter and shot the man down. Some claim that Plummer lived in fear of Cleveland and suspected that the man would eventually cause trouble for him.

As the number of lawmen chasing the Plummer Gang increased, the outlaws were having more difficulty staying out of their reach. A major problem associated with fleeing pursuers was related to the fact that Plummer insisted on transporting the huge load of stolen gold ingots, coins, and nuggets by mule wherever he went instead of caching the hoard somewhere. In time, the mule train of riches grew to four animals, and because the overburdened and recalcitrant mules made escape difficult, the outlaws often found themselves overtaken by pursuers and forced into shootouts. The gang members constantly complained about the slow-moving pack animals, but Plummer ignored them, reminding them that he was in charge. At one point, Cleveland threatened to shoot the mules if Plummer didn't come up with a better plan for taking care of the booty. It was estimated that Plummer's share of the fortune during this time was worth well over $1 million.

Successful robberies became more and more difficult and Plummer and his gang members had become all too well-known by lawmen and citizens throughout much of northern Idaho. Because they were now recognized everywhere they traveled in the area, Plummer decided they needed to move their operation someplace else. He selected Montana.

During the autumn of 1862, the Plummer Gang arrived in the tiny settlement of Sun River, Montana, 20 miles east of Great Falls. The outlaws liked what they found in the area and decided it would serve as a suitable base of operations. They moved into an abandoned ranch house that Plummer had found a short distance out of town. Once the outlaws settled in, Plummer counted out amounts of gold from the treasure carried by the mules and paid each member of the gang. Plummer kept the largest portion for himself, a decision that was met with hostility. The gang members grew upset and told Plummer that they had been under the impression that all of the gold was to be split equally, making each of them wealthy men. Plummer explained to them that, as leader of the gang, the gold was his and that the men were only working for him and thus paid accordingly.

The most vocal dissenter was Cleveland, who insisted that he had stolen more of the gold than Plummer and that at least half of it should be his. Though furious, Cleveland, along with the other gang members, settled for the relatively small payment offered by Plummer, but none were happy about it.

After the gang had been in Sun River for several weeks, Plummer informed then that he was going to travel to the gold fields near the town of Bannock, Idaho, in order to determine if the area would be suitable to carry out more robberies. As Plummer was loading his gold onto his mules, several of the gang members approached and informed him that they didn't like the idea of him riding away with that much loot, part of which they thought should belong to them. As a compromise, Plummer agreed to let one of the gang members accompany him to Bannock. The men chose Cleveland.

During the trip, Plummer and Cleveland rarely spoke, their animosity for each other apparent. Plummer was convinced that Cleveland planned to kill him and take all of the gold for himself. As a result, he got little sleep and was irritable and nervous the entire time they were in Bannock. Nothing was accomplished, and the two men, along with the mules transporting over $1 million in gold, returned to Sun River.

When the two outlaws arrived at the hideout, they discovered that the other gang members had ridden into Great Falls for some drinking and gambling. When Cleveland went into the house, Plummer unloaded the gold from the mules, removed the packsaddles, and unbridled the animals and turned them out into the pasture. Plummer then went into the house and poured a drink for himself and for Cleveland.

Plummer retrieved a deck of cards from his saddlebags and invited Cleveland to play a game or two. As the two men played, Plummer made certain that Cleveland's glass was always filled with whiskey, while he himself only pretended to drink. After about two hours, Cleveland was drunk and passed out on the table. While he was asleep, Plummer carried the packs of gold down to a small nearby creek some 200 yards from the ranch house and buried them.

The next morning, when the two men awoke, Plummer told Cleveland that he was going to ride back to Bannock to re-evaluate the possibilities for conducting the robberies. Cleveland insisted on going along and saddled his horse. When Plummer rode up a few minutes later, ready to depart but without the pack-laden mules, Cleveland asked him where the gold was. Plummer told the outlaw that he had hidden it in a safe place. Enraged, Cleveland pulled a revolver, leveled it at Plummer, and threatened to kill him. A second later, Plummer drew his own weapon and shot Cleveland, killing him instantly. Without a second look at the dead outlaw, Plummer spurred his horse past the dead man and rode on to Bannock.

After spending a few days in the Idaho town, Plummer discovered that the opportunities to amass a fortune by stealing were great. While he made plans to accumulate more gold and add to his already immense fortune, Plummer ingratiated himself with local businessmen and politicians. Weeks later, in May 1863, Plummer somehow managed to get elected sheriff of Bannock. Shortly after taking office, he returned to Sun River and met with his gang members. He made each of them deputies and returned with them to Bannock.

Days later, Plummer returned to Sun River, where he courted and married a woman named Electa Bryan. The two of them traveled to Bannock and moved into a small-frame house in town. Years later, when she was an elderly woman, Electa told a newspaper reporter that Plummer had told her about the large fortune in gold ingots, coins, and nuggets that he had buried next to a small creek at Sun River, and that he had never had an opportunity to return to the location and retrieve it.

Plummer, as sheriff, along with his deputized gang members, used his position to steal and confiscate gold from the many miners and freight companies in the area. If anyone opposed him, Plummer either had them killed or killed them himself. During the six-month period when Plummer was sheriff of Bannock, he and his men were responsible for 102 murders and uncountable robberies.

As had become his custom, Plummer loaded his stolen gold onto mules and led them everywhere he traveled. When the packs were full, Plummer, alone, led the mules to remote locations near Bannock, where he buried them. Plummer never told anyone where he had hidden his gold and, as far as anyone knows, never left a map or directions indicating the location of his caches.

In addition to the huge cache located near the small stream close to the ranch house near Sun River, Plummer is known to have cached over $200,000 near Birdtail Rock on the Mullin Road during the time he returned to Sun River to marry Electa. A short time after his wedding, Plummer and his gang held up a stagecoach near Deer Lodge, Montana, took $50,000 worth of gold, and buried it within hours somewhere along the bank of Cottonwood Creek. Near Cascade, a few miles south of Sun River, Plummer reportedly buried $300,000 in gold not far from the old St. Peter's Mission. History records that Plummer was executed before returning to any of his valuable caches. Electa verified this observation, stating that none of them were ever retrieved by the outlaw.

It did not take long for the citizens and businessmen of Bannock to grow weary over Plummer's reign of terror and theft. Secret meetings were held by the townsfolk, who discussed ways to rid themselves of the crooked sheriff and his gang. A vigilante committee was organized and armed, and their charge was to rid the region of Plummer and his influence. One at a time, individual members of his gang were tracked down, apprehended, and hanged. Others, realizing their days were numbered, fled Bannock, never to return. On January 10, 1864, the vigilantes caught up with Plummer and with little fanfare hanged him, bringing to an end his vicious depredations throughout the region.

Some who have studied the life and times of Henry Plummer have suggested that a number of the townsfolk of Bannock were jealous of the outlaw's success and coveted his great wealth. They felt, it has been suggested, that in eliminating him they might somehow come into possession of the vast amount of gold he was known to possess. Some have maintained that the vigilantes themselves were little better than the gang of outlaws led by Plummer. A number of eyewitnesses reported that prior to hanging him, several of the vigilantes forced Plummer to reveal the location of at least one of his gold caches. Whether this is true or not has never been verified, but it remained a fact that a few members of the vigilante committee became wealthy only a few days after Plummer's execution.

In 1869, Electa Plummer returned to Sun River with a map that reputedly showed the location of the massive fortune in gold ingots, coins, and nuggets buried there by her late husband. Though she searched for days, she was unable to locate the treasure. Some who knew her were convinced that she was unable to interpret the rather cryptic map she carried and thus that she searched in the wrong places. What became of this map is unknown.

A stepson of one of the surviving Plummer Gang members was 12 years old in 1875, when he was playing along a shallow creek not far from the old Sun River ranch house once used by the outlaws. The stepson, whose name was Henry Ford, was digging in the soft soil of the bank next to the stream when, to his great surprise, he unearthed several very old leather sacks filled with small gold ingots. He dragged one of the sacks home and showed his stepfather, who recognized the ingots and estimated their value at around $60,000. Several days later, the stepfather, realizing that the sack of gold bars was only a fraction of the treasure Plummer was known to have hidden, asked Henry to lead him back to the location where he had found the gold bars. The two returned to the area, but the boy was unable to relocate the hole he had dug. Though they searched the area for hours, they were unable to find anything.

In 1890, a man named Jack Young arrived at Sun River. His mother, he claimed, was the sister of one of Plummer's gang members. She had been in the possession of a crudely drawn map that she believed showed where Henry Plummer had buried his huge gold cache near the creek. She turned the map over to Young and, following it, he came to a location not far from where Henry Ford claimed that he had found the leather sack 14 years earlier. After several minutes of digging into the soil of the creek bank, Young uncovered more leather sacks filled with small gold ingots.

These are the only recorded instances of any portion of Henry Plummer's loot being found. Though substantial, the sacks of gold ingots found near Sun River represent only a fraction of the wealth the outlaw buried at or near this location. Most researchers are convinced that the bulk of the treasure still lies buried nearby.

In addition to this site, it is estimated that Plummer buried the loot from other robberies in as many as six other locations throughout Idaho and Montana – locations treasure hunters are still searching for.

Chapter 15

Outlaw Cy Skinner's Buried Loot

Noted California outlaw Cyrus Skinner was born in Ohio. As a teenager, he and his brother George traveled to Texas to try to make their living. After getting into trouble, the two fled to California, arriving in 1850. They went under the aliases Cyrus and George Williamson. In the Golden State, the brothers lost no time in finding trouble once again. Following charges of burglary and grand larceny, George managed to escape but Cyrus was arrested, tried, and sentenced to the penitentiary at San Quentin. For reasons that are unclear, he was released six months later but found himself in hot water again on another grand larceny charge in Yuba County. He was sentenced to prison once again, this time for three years, but escaped after serving only four months.

When his brother George was released several months later, the Skinner brothers joined the Richard Barter Gang.

Barter and his toughs terrorized the miners around Nevada City, California, raiding their camps and taking their hard-earned gold. George Skinner was killed a short time later but the Barter Gang, with Cyrus still a member, turned to robbing stagecoaches. Following one such robbery, Barter and Skinner found themselves trapped in a mountain pass by a pursuing posse. Barter was killed and Skinner arrested. Once again, he was sent to San Quentin prison. There he met and became friends with Henry Plummer, who was serving a term for murder.

Skinner spent 15 years in prison before escaping in August 1859. Shortly thereafter, he ran into Plummer in Lewiston, Montana. Together, the two men formed a gang and set about robbing travelers, freight wagons, and stagecoaches. Over time, the gang accumulated an impressive amount of loot in the form of gold and silver coins. When Plummer was captured and hanged on January 10, 1864, Cyrus Skinner became aware that law enforcement authorities, as well as vigilante committees, were closing in. He decided it was time to get away from the region as quickly as possible.

Within minutes of hearing of Plummer's death, Skinner had stuffed gold dust, nuggets, and coins – his share from numerous robberies – into ore sacks and saddlebags. In addition to his own gold, Skinner also packed tens of thousands of dollars' worth of loot that had belonged to some other gang members, now all dead. After loading the booty onto two mules, Skinner, joined by six surviving gang members, fled in the dark of night. The nervous outlaws traveled to the settlement of Hell's Gate (now Missoula), near the eastern border of Montana.

Once at Hell's Gate, Skinner sought out an old friend named Bill Hamilton. Hamilton lived a small cabin on the edge of town, was known to members of the Plummer Gang, and could be depended on to provide sanctuary to those fleeing from the law. Skinner moved in with Hamilton during the third week of January 1864.

Skinner knew that it would only be a matter of time before law enforcement officers learned of his whereabouts, so he made plans to travel north into Canada. Skinner determined that the two mule loads of gold would slow his escape, so he decided to bury the hoard someplace near Hell's Gate and return for it later. Riding up and down the banks of the Missoula River, Skinner examined the many small islands visible in the middle of the stream. Electing one he believed was suitable, he recruited two gang members, Robert English and Louis Crossette, to help him bury the gold.

The three outlaws crossed a portion of Clarks Fork and arrived at one of the small islands in the middle of a cold January night. After stuffing the dust and nuggets into three large cast-iron kettles and the coins into a brass water bucket, they dug a hole near the center of the island, placed the loot within, covered it, and returned to Hamilton's cabin.

A few days after burying the gold, Skinner and the remaining members of the gang learned that the law had discovered they were hiding out at Hell's Gate and that preparations were underway to arrest them. Crossette, who was part Blackfoot Indian, packed his few belongings and went to live with his tribe. Years later, Crossette often spoke of his desire to return to the island in the middle of the Missoula River and retrieving Skinner's gold, but before he could do so, he was stabbed to death in a saloon fight.

Robert English fled to California, where he returned to his old occupation of robbing stagecoaches. After several brushes with the law over the next 10 years, English finally retired from outlawry.

Skinner mistakenly believed he would be safe hiding out at Hamilton's cabin until the spring thaw. On the afternoon of January 26, however, vigilantes rode up to the cabin, dragged Skinner out to a nearby creek, and hanged him from the limb of a cottonwood tree. Aware that Skinner had fled Bannock with a fortune in gold, the vigilantes searched Hamilton's cabin and the adjacent property for it but found nothing. With the hanging of Skinner, the only man left alive who knew about the gold was Robert English.

Years later, when most citizens of Montana had long since forgotten about Henry Plummer, Cyrus Skinner, and other outlaws, Robert English returned to Hell's Gate. By this time, he had changed his name to Charley Duchase. After arriving, English spent several days riding along the Missoula River searching for the island on which he, Skinner, and Crossette had buried the gold, but many years had passed, and such changes had occurred in the river and its islands that he was unable to determine the correct one. The former outlaw noted that the river had changed its course somewhat. He also believed that there were more islands than had existed back in 1864. In truth, English was inspecting the river during a time when stream flow was low, thus exposing more islands than normally encountered. Confused and uncertain, English eventually abandoned his search for the buried treasure and returned to California.

In 1894, a man arrived in Missoula from St. Paul, Minnesota, to search for Skinner's gold. He possessed an old map that he claimed showed the location of the buried treasure on one of the islands in the Missoula River. For several weeks the man rowed out to the various islands and excavated numerous holes but found nothing.

During the 1930s, a man named E. Taichert, a longtime Missoula resident, learned the story of Cyrus Skinner's lost gold cache. For years thereafter, Taichert collected and studied every fragment of information he could find concerning the tale. Finally, Taichert was certain he knew the exact island in which the treasure was buried.

Selecting the third island downstream from the bridge that leads to Montana State University, Taichert waited until the stream flow was lower than normal. One night, he gathered up his pick and shovel, waded the river, and proceeded to excavate in an area at one end of the island. While digging the third hole, Taichert's shovel struck a metal bucket about six inches below the surface. Excited, he removed the bucket and refilled the hole. Returning home, he examined the contents of the bucket and was delighted to discover that it contained several thousand dollars' worth of gold coins. Taichert was convinced that he had located the Skinner cache. He began to make plans to return to the island the next evening and retrieve the rest of it.

That evening, however, heavy rains caused the river to rise. The next morning, when Taichert arrived at the riverbank, he discovered that the stream was near flood-stage and all of the islands were underwater. The river remained high and swift for nearly two weeks, delaying Taichert's search. Finally, the water level subsided and he was able to return to the island, only to discover its configuration had been altered as a result of the raging floodwaters. For several days he examined the island, dug holes, and poked around, but he was unable to locate the exact site from which he had earlier removed the iron bucket.

Weeks passed, and Taichert received an opportunity to invest in a mining enterprise in Lincoln, about 60 miles east of Missoula. After disposing of the coins he had discovered, Taichert purchased an interest in the mine, bought some equipment, and left Missoula.

In 1957, Taichert retired and returned to Missoula. For the next six years, he rowed out to the third island from the bridge and searched for Skinner's gold at every opportunity. Finally, in 1963, when he was 80 years old, he abandoned the search.

Taichert believed, as did many others, that the greatest portion of outlaw Skinner's gold remained buried on the island – and therein lies the problem. Because the rising and falling river alternately erodes material from one end of the island and deposits it at the other, the process constantly changing the island's shape. Taichert believed that maps purporting to show the location of the treasure were useless.

Skinner's gold, worth well over $2 million today, is believed to still be concealed beneath a foot or so of sand and gravel on a small island in the middle of the Missoula River.

Chapter 16

The Deathbed Confession
of Alton Baker

During the summer of 1942, an elderly man named Alton Baker lay dying in a Eugene, Oregon, hospital ward. Though ravaged by old age and all of its accompanying infirmities, it was obvious that the old man had been healthy and robust in his younger days and had apparently led most of his life in the out-of-doors. One of the attending nurses remarked that Baker "looked like a man with a history and not all of it good." Baker seldom spoke, revealed nothing about himself, and only asked when he might be able to leave the hospital.

It was not to happen. The doctors told Baker that he had not long to live and that nothing could be done for him. Several days after receiving this information, Baker, with a look of haunted desperation in his eyes, summoned a young male hospital orderly and instructed him to sit by his bedside, telling him that he needed to get some things told. Over the next two hours, the orderly heard the incredible tale of an outlaw past and a hidden treasure, along with the bizarre circumstances that surrounded it.

During the 1870s, Alton Baker prowled the trails leading into and out of Grants Pass, Oregon, and earned his living by robbing stagecoaches and travelers. In the company of two fellow outlaws, he preyed on the unarmed, the weak, and the unsuspecting. Over time, Baker amassed an impressive fortune in gold and cash.

One day, Baker and his companions learned about a large gold shipment as it was passing through the town of Woodville (now Rogue River) and headed for San Francisco. Pulling along three packhorses, the outlaws waited at a pre-selected location along the trail. As the coach approached, they rode out into the road and ordered the driver to pull to a halt. After tying up the driver and the guard, Baker and his men broke open the large, heavy chests carrying the gold and transferred the shipment into saddlebags that they lashed onto the mules and their own horses. Riding away from the scene of the crime, the three bandits traveled several miles before turning into the drainage basin of Foots Creek, a location they had settled on days earlier. Once deep into Foots Creek Canyon, the riders stopped at the entrance to an old mine tunnel, into which they cached the gold.

That evening, while finishing dinner around a campfire, the three outlaws entered into a discussion related to the division of the loot. Unhappy with his share, one of the bandits drew his revolver and issued threats. He was immediately shot dead by Baker and the other outlaw. As he regarded the corpse on the ground before them, Baker turned and shot and killed the surviving partner, thereby maintaining possession all of the loot for himself. As Baker related this part of the tale to the hospital orderly, tears welled up in his aged eyes and he wondered aloud how he could ever be forgiven for such a cowardly act.

In the light of a full moon, Baker dragged the two dead men into the abandoned mine shaft and, after several trips, moved the gold to a different location. He buried it at the base of an old madroña tree. He completed the task an hour before sunrise.

When the morning sun finally illuminated the shallow canyon, Baker broke camp, packed his gear onto his horse, and made preparations to leave. He intended to return in one year when he believed the threat of pursuit by lawmen had diminished. After turning the other horses and mules loose, he regarded the madroña tree where he had buried the gold. Since it looked like several others that grew in this canyon, Baker decided to mark it. Casting about the campsite, he located a broken saddle horn that he wedged into a fork in the tree before riding away to California.

As Baker spent his days in Sacramento, he fell into the habit of drinking every evening at an establishment called the Glitter Tavern. One night, he found himself involved in an argument with a fellow patron and, during an ensuing scuffle, stabbed him to death. Baker was arrested, tried, convicted, and given a life sentence in a California state prison.

As Baker languished in the penitentiary, his dreams were often filled with visions of the fortune in gold cached at the base of the madroña tree in faraway Foots Creek Canyon. At times, the images of his dead partners would intrude during his sleep and he would jerk awake, screaming.

Years passed, and Baker, a model prisoner, was eventu-

Mr. Prefontaine told the orderly that he had been deep in Foots Creek Canyon on several occasions and knew exactly where the old mine shaft was located. Furthermore, he said, he recalled once encountering a large, old madroña tree with a busted saddle horn wedged into a fork about chest-high. Moments later, the two men were hiking up into the canyon, eager to locate the long-lost cache of gold.

Prefontaine had no trouble relocating the old mine shaft and led the orderly straight to it. Since his last visit to the tunnel several years earlier, however, it had caved in. Several yards away, at the foot of a gentle slope extending from the opening of the mine, lay a grove of madroña trees. Though the two men searched among the trees for over an hour, they could not find the one with the broken saddle horn. Prefontaine ventured the opinion that the old wooden horn had simply rotted away and fallen from its perch.

Discouraged, the two men returned to the cabin. As sundown approached, the orderly and his wife bade goodbye to the Prefontaines and drove away, never to return. Prefontaine, however, could not stop from thinking about the story of the buried stagecoach treasure. He returned to the madroña grove many times over the next few years in the hope of finding some clue as to which tree grew next to the cache. Though he excavated at several locations, he found nothing.

Eventually, Prefontaine tired of his search and gave up hope of ever locating Alton Baker's buried treasure. During the 1950s, however, he read a magazine article that introduced him to metal detectors, and he decided that one of these machines had the potential to locate the buried gold. Prefontaine purchased one of the instruments from a mail-order catalog. After it was delivered, he familiarized himself with its operation and, with great anticipation, carried it into the canyon and to the grove of trees.

On arriving at the location, Prefontaine was surprised and disappointed to discover that a fire had ravaged the madroña grove, burning it away entirely. Furthermore, and equally discouraging, a subsequent flood had covered much of the area with a deposit of stream gravel and silt. Nothing looked the same. Using his new metal detector, Prefontaine scanned the ground where he believed the madroña grove to have been, but he received no positive signals from the instrument.

Discouraged once again, Prefontaine decided to give up the search for the buried treasure for good. Since he was now elderly and in failing health, it was the last time he was ever to visit the canyon.

Estimates of the value of the gold buried by Alton Baker in Foots Creek Canyon range from $20,000 to $150,000 in 1870s values. If found today, this remarkable cache would be worth a sizeable fortune.

Chapter 17

Ella Watson's Buried Fortune

Not only do outlaws come in all shapes and sizes, they come from different backgrounds, occupations, races, and ethnic groups. They also come in different genders. Female outlaws were more common in the historical American west than many realize, and are exemplified by the likes of Belle Starr, Pearl Hart, and others. One of the worst was Ella Watson, who was widely experienced in robbery, livestock rustling, and a variety of hustles and cons. Before she was hanged in the summer of 1899, Watson buried $50,000 worth of gold and silver coins near her residence in the Sweetwater River Valley of southeastern Wyoming.

Ella Watson was not the kind of woman normally found in frontier Wyoming. She was a large, boisterous woman, a dead shot, and could hold her own with any man. After running away from her family's Kansas farm when she was 15,

tivities and learned that she had buried more than $50,000 worth of gold and silver coins in a secret location near the cabin. The man told her that if she turned the money over to them, she and Averill would be set free. Averill, listening in on the conversation, hissed at Watson and told her to keep quiet about the cache. He assured her that the men were only bluffing and that no harm would come to them.

A few minutes later, the wagon pulled up under a large, spreading cottonwood tree. As two of the men prepared nooses, Averill and Watson were pulled to a standing position in the back of the wagon. The ropes were tossed over a low-hanging limb and the nooses placed over the heads of the prisoners. The leader of the cattlemen repeated the offer to spare the lives of Watson and Averill if they would reveal the location of the buried gold and silver coins. By this time, Watson had grown quite frightened and was about to reveal the location of the cache, but Averill once again insisted that nothing was going to happen to them and that the men were just trying to scare them.

After the nooses were tightened around the necks of the man and woman, the men jumped from the wagon, leaving the two cattle thieves standing side-by-side at the ends of the ropes. For the third time, the offer to spare them in exchange for the location of the buried coins was advanced, and for the third time it was refused. At that point, one of the cattlemen lashed at the flanks of the wagon's team of horses, causing the vehicle to bolt way. A second later, Ella Watson and Jim Averill were swinging under the cottonwood limb, their lives being slowly choked away by the constricting nooses. Within a few more seconds, they were dead.

The cattlemen returned to Watson's cabin and retrieved their livestock. While four of them drove the cattle toward the east, two remained to search the property for the buried cache of coins. They found nothing. Over the years others, on hearing the story of Ella Watson and her buried fortune, many have made the trip to the long-abandoned cabin to search for the gold and silver they knew to be buried somewhere nearby. No evidence has ever surfaced that it has been found.

Thirty years after the hanging of Ella Watson and Jim Averill, a letter from Watson to her family in Smith County, Kanas, was discovered in an old trunk. The letter, apparently written only a few weeks before her death, detailed her rustling activities and her love affair with Averill. Clearly trying to impress the relatives she had fled years earlier, Watson, in a nearly illegible scrawl, told of the money she had earned from stealing cattle and how she had hidden her fortune in an abandoned, shallow well near the cabin. Watson's letter, discovered in 1929, eventually came into the possession of a man who was familiar with the Sweetwater River country and the tales of long-ago cattle rustling activities. He also knew the location of the old cabin in which Watson lived.

Weeks later, when he arrived at the site of the cabin, he was disappointed to discover that it had been torn down and the surrounding land turned into pasture. Though he searched for hours, he could find no evidence of an abandoned well. With the passage of time, it had apparently been filled in and grown over with grass.

As far as is known, the gold and silver coins hidden by Ella Watson over a century ago still lie several feet below the surface. Today, the $50,000 in coins that were buried during the 1890s would be worth considerably more. If the old abandoned well could ever be located, the finder would not have to work another day in his or her life.

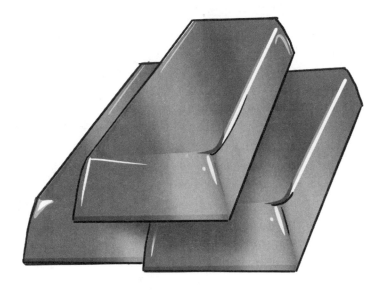

Chapter 18

The Priest's Gold Ingots

Most people would likely think that the last person to turn to outlawry would be a priest, but the truth is that throughout history, holy men have occasionally crossed the threshold of one chosen profession into another, for one that held the attraction of great wealth. One such example is a priest-turned-bandit named LaFarge, his first name lost to history.

LaFarge was a native of France and a man with a troubled past. At one point in his life, he was admitted to the priesthood and assigned to central Mexico, where his duties included converting the natives and putting them to work tending fields and raising goats. Though the exact details are unknown, Padre LaFarge was convicted of killing a nun. He was defrocked and sentenced to prison. Several years later, he was released, but continued to assume the role of a priest, wearing the robe and hood of a Catholic friar.

LaFarge drifted northward to the Rio Grande, traveling from settlement to settlement and using his disguise to his advantage. Posing as a poor holy man on a journey to save souls, LaFarge was always treated with respect, fed, and provided shelter. During his travels, he fell in with six other Frenchmen he encountered along the way. Many weeks later, they arrived in Taos, New Mexico, where they established a placer mining operation along several of the small mountain streams found in the area. None of the men had any mining experience, and they soon became frustrated with their meager take from the gold-laden streams. Even more frustrating was news of the large amounts of gold panned by the miners nearby. The Frenchmen decided it would be easier to take the gold from the successful miners than to continue the drudgery of panning for their own. Over the next several weeks, the seven Frenchmen robbed and killed 22 miners and accumulated a large store of stolen gold. At this point, LaFarge hired a man named Jose Lopat, a Spaniard who had experience in smelting gold ore and forming it into ingots.

From the stolen gold, Lopat molded 500 gold bars, each a small hand-sized ingot. This done, LaFarge decided it would be best to take what they had accumulated and quit the area before their deeds were discovered. He decided it would be best to transport the gold along the old Santa Fe Trail for a distance and then head south to New Orleans. There, they, along with the gold, would travel back to their homeland, where they could all live a life of luxury with their newly acquired wealth. Lopat remained in the employ of the Frenchmen as a guide. Four Indians were convinced to accompany the Frenchmen as hired workers, but they were little more than slaves.

Weeks later, the slow-moving party labored along a point of the trail in what today is the Oklahoma Panhandle. Lopat, who had ridden ahead to scout, returned with the information that there was a spring ahead and that, as it was nearing sundown, it would serve as an ideal place to camp for the night. Both LaFarge and Lopat noted the presence of a prominent feature of the landscape a short distance to the north: a rounded elevation that, years later, acquired the name "Sugar Loaf Mountain." When the party arrived at the spring, they found four mountain men camped there. The men were transporting a load of furs from a recent trapping expedition. On learning the Frenchmen's plans, the trappers told them that New Orleans no longer belonged to France and that it had been sold to the United States. LaFarge grew concerned that the U. S. government would never allow them to ship the ingots out of the country and might even confiscate them. Secretly, he confided his concerns to his fellows, and they decided to send two of their number on to New Orleans to arrange for a vessel to meet them somewhere along the coast, far from the scrutiny of government agents.

The following morning, two of the Frenchmen departed for the Crescent City while LaFarge and the rest of the party prepared for a long stay at the spring. It was estimated that it would take three and a half months to make the round trip, so LaFarge ordered the Indian slaves to build several dugouts and rock dwellings for shelter against the approaching winter.

By the end of December, the two Frenchmen had not returned. LaFarge decided to bury the gold bars until he could determine the best way to ship them to France. He ordered Lopat and the Indians to return to Santa Fe. Once they were out of sight, he buried the gold ingots, presumably in the vicinity of the spring. Today this water source is known as

Flagg Spring and is located in the north-central part of Cimarron County, Oklahoma.

On returning to Santa Fe, Lopat somehow learned of LaFarge's criminal past. He wrote down what he had learned, as well as his account of helping the Frenchmen transport the gold to Flagg Spring in the back of his family Bible. It is this chronicle in the handwriting of Jose Lopat that provides most of the information about the gold ingots of Padre LaFarge.

Several more months passed, and Lopat spotted the robed and hooded figure of LaFarge walking down a Santa Fe street. LaFarge told Lopat that the others had been killed by Indians and that only he, LaFarge, knew the location of the buried gold. He informed Lopat that he was preparing an expedition to return to Flagg Spring to retrieve the gold and invited him to serve once again as guide. Lopat suspected that LaFarge had killed the others and would likely murder him once he had acquired the ingots. LaFarge told Lopat that he would be well paid for his services, but the Spaniard said he wanted to consider the offer for a few days.

While Lopat stalled, LaFarge was identified by two men as a member of the group that had raided and killed the placer miners months earlier. Several townspeople were enlisted, and soon a mob roamed the streets of Santa Fe in search of the outlaw priest. LaFarge escaped for a time by hiding under some baggage in an ox cart, but he was eventually discovered and captured several miles outside of Santa Fe. Two weeks later, Lopat learned that Lafarge had been killed and buried in an unmarked grave out on the plains.

Buried with LaFarge was the secret of the location of the 500 buried gold ingots. Based on what LaFarge had told him, Lopat believed he could find them. He made a trip to Flagg Spring, but found no evidence that the gold had been buried anywhere in the vicinity.

The story of the lost gold of Padre LaFarge evolved into legend over the next few decades. No record has been found of any organized attempt to locate the buried treasure. In 1870, a series of strange stone markers were discovered near the old Spanish trail. The markers consisted of huge stones rolled into place to form the shapes of Vs. Each V pointed toward the next marker, which was always five to 10 miles away. The strange stone direction markers, as they were called, were found in a somewhat regular pattern from Santa Fe to the settlement of Las Vegas, New Mexico, nearly 50 miles away. Beyond Las Vegas, searchers were unable to locate any other markers. Several years later, however, more of the stone markers was discovered along the old road to Clayton, New Mexico, in the northeastern part of the state, and just a few miles west of the tip of the Oklahoma Panhandle.

Then, in 1900, a rancher named Ryan was driving a herd of recently purchased horses from Clayton to his ranch in Cimarron County. One evening, several horses wandered away from an encampment and scattered out onto the plains. Ryan began a search the next morning and, after a few hours of tracking, stopped to rest. As he was smoking a cigarette and regarding the countryside, he spotted another of the stone markers. It consisted of large rocks like all the others and was in the distinct shape of a large V. Ryan, who was familiar with the legend of the lost gold ingots of Padre LaFarge, was convinced that these man-made arrangements of small boulders pointed the way to the buried treasure.

Over the next two years, Ryan searched for and found several more of the markers. They led him to the general vicinity of Flagg Spring. Ryan searched the area of the spring for several years but was never able to locate the cache.

Ryan's great-nephew, a man named Cy Strong, whose ranch was located in the shadow of Sugar Loaf Mountain, was certain the ingots were buried somewhere near the spring. Not far from the spring, Strong found the remains of an ancient dugout as well as a jumble of rocks and weathered adobe bricks that apparently composed part of a crude dwelling. In addition, several pieces of rotted oxcart wheels were found nearby. More recently, however, Strong discovered other stone markers that suggested the treasure might have been buried closer to Sugar Loaf Mountain. Subsequent searches there by Strong failed to locate anything of significance.

Since the turn of the century, untold numbers of treasure hunters have arrived at Flagg Spring to search for the hidden gold of Padre LaFarge. Some come armed with maps, others carry sophisticated metal detectors, all to no avail. Current gold prices would place the value of the gold at millions of dollars. This tantalizing figure has inspired a group of treasure hunters to employ a low-level hot-air balloon to search for additional stone markers in the vicinity of Flagg Spring and Sugar Loaf Mountain. They suggest that some important directional information that might elude searchers on the ground might be found via low altitude surveillance. Some residents of Cimarron County believe it will just be a matter of time before the secret location of the gold ingots is revealed.

Chapter 19

Chief Victorio's Lost Gold

While they are seldom placed in the context of American outlaws, some of the most efficient and successful bandits in our history were American Indians. One of the worst, if accounts of the time are to be believed, was the Apache chief Victorio. It can be argued that Victorio conducted more robberies and raids, stole more gold, and killed more men than all of the rest of America's noted outlaws combined.

Victorio, born in 1825, was a noted warrior and chief of the Warm Springs Apaches. During his lifetime, Victorio led raids on small villages and ranches both in the American Southwest and in Mexico. He attacked wagon trains, stagecoaches, and solitary travelers. He looted churches and missions. In the process, this fearsome warrior accumulated a huge amount of gold and silver in the form of ingots and coins as well as gold crosses, chalices, and other items. In the process, Victorio and his warriors killed many, and most roads and trails throughout parts of West Texas, New Mexico, and Arizona were deemed dangerous during his reign. The Apache had little personal use for gold save for fashioning ornaments on rare occasions. The precious metal could, however, purchase needed firearms and ammunition, and Victorio was aware that white people were covetous of gold and silver. In time, Victorio acquired so much gold that he found it necessary to hide it in secret places. He was killed before he could return to his caches.

One day in 1929, a high school teacher in Ysleta, Texas, by the name of Myrtle Love received a telephone call from the El Paso County sheriff, who knew of her interest in the legends and lore of West Texas. The sheriff told her that there was a man in the county jail who had a very interesting tale to tell and that he would arrange a meeting with the man if she so desired. The man's name was Race Compton, and he had been found sleeping in a boxcar at the railroad yard. As he had no money on his person and bore the general appearance of a hobo, he was charged with vagrancy. When Miss Love was admitted to the small interview room, she found an elderly man, probably in his late sixties, who had the weatherworn appearance of one who had spent the better part of his life outdoors. He was bewhiskered and had gone many weeks without a haircut. His hands were calloused and hard from years of hard work, but they were steady. Compton was well-mannered and, in measured tones, explained to Miss Love how he came to be in El Paso.

He was there, he said, to obtain some dynamite and digging equipment, which he needed to gain entry to a cave that had had been sealed up and reputedly contained millions of dollars' worth of gold. As Compton spoke, Myrtle Love recorded the following story.

In 1859, the Butterfield Stage Line was doing a brisk business. Coaches passed through West Texas carrying mail, payroll, and sometimes gold in the form of ingots and nuggets. Throughout the Trans-Pecos region, a network of stations had been established to provide fresh horses for the coaches and meals for the passengers and drivers. One such station had been built at Eagle Springs, Texas, located in the northern foothills of the Eagle Mountains, 15 miles northwest of Van Horn and 12 miles northeast of Indian Hot Springs, on the Rio Grande.

Bigfoot Wallace, who later gained fame as a daring and adventurous Texas Ranger, was a driver on one of these coaches. His partner was Joe Peacock, a 19-year-old who, despite his age, had already been involved in a number of skirmishes with outlaws and Indians and had killed several men. During that time, Apache raiders were active in this part of West Texas, and Chief Victorio, the bloodthirsty leader of the Warm Springs band, had a reputation for hating white people.

Within moments after the stagecoach pulled into the Eagle Springs station, Victorio and a band of some 20 warriors charged out of the mountains and attacked. Two of the passengers and one of the men who operated the station were killed, several horses were stolen, and Peacock, who had been impaled in the leg by an arrow, was taken captive by the raiders. Traveling day and night without stopping, the Indians rode south, crossed the Rio Grande, and made their way to their stronghold in the Tres Castillos Mountains in northern Chihuahua. Here, they felt safe from pursuit by the U. S. Cavalry and Texas Rangers.

Peacock had his wound treated by a young Apache girl called Juanita, who was said to be the daughter of Victorio. His wound was not serious and in a matter of a few days he was able to walk. He was put to work in the Indian camp gathering firewood and performing other tasks normally reserved for women and slaves.

During the several months Peacock remained a prisoner of the Apaches, Juanita became attracted to him. On several occasions, Victorio threated to kill the white man but each time, Juanita begged for his life to be spared. Eventually, young Peacock was allowed to go about his camp duties without a guard, as escape from this mountain stronghold was virtually impossible.

At night, Peacock and Juanita would meet secretly. Displaying uncharacteristic boldness for an Apache woman, Juanita tried to persuade Peacock to become her husband. Peacock was cautious; he did not want to refuse Juanita and chance the wrath of a rejected woman who thus far was the only reason he was still alive. He managed to stall, stating that he was very concerned about his mother back in Texas and needed to see that she was safe and well cared for. Juanita accepted this explanation but continued to pressure the young Texan. One night she told him that if he would agree to become her husband, she would tell him where Chief Victorio hid his stolen gold. The notion of a fortune in gold intrigued Peacock.

During his imprisonment, Peacock had watched the Apaches come and go with stolen ingots of gold as well as pouches of nuggets. He learned that the gold was taken from freight wagons and pack trains that were attacked by the Indians. He knew they often carried the gold into Mexico, where they traded it for rifles and ammunition. On occasion, Peacock would watch as a tribal artisan hammered out a golden amulet or some other item of jewelry.

When Peacock asked Juanita about the gold, she told

him that it was kept in a cave with a small opening in the Eagle Mountains, not far from where he was captured near the stagecoach station. One could get to it, she said, from the old Indian trail that led from Eagle Springs through the mountains toward Indian Hot Springs on the Rio Grande. Juanita said she had been in the cave many times with her father and remembered seeing dozens of gold bars stacked against the back wall. In addition, she said, there were numerous buckskin pouches containing gold coins and nuggets. She said it would require 50 mules to transport all of the gold that was stored in the cave.

Juanita also told Peacock that a few days earlier, Victorio and several warriors had been on their way to the cave when they had encountered a contingent of cavalry. There had been a brief skirmish, during which one Indian was wounded and two of the soldiers were killed. The Indians went on to the cave to remove a small amount of gold. This done, Victorio, fearing that the whites were close to discovering the location of the cache of gold, ordered his braves to conceal the entrance by plugging it with a number of large rocks such that it looked no different from the rest of the mountainside. Being familiar with the area Juanita described, Peacock was convinced that he could locate the cave with little difficulty. That night, he began to formulate plans for an escape.

Several weeks passed and no opportunity for escape was afforded Peacock. Then one day, Victorio and a large contingent of warriors left for a major raiding expedition deep into Chihuahua, leaving only women, children, and old men in the Tres Castillos camp. That night Peacock met again with Juanita, told her of his plans to leave, and promised to return for her as soon as he could. She obtained a horse for him and provided him with a deer gut full of water and a pouch filled with jerked meat. In the dark of night, Peacock made his way out of the mountains and across the desert. Several days later, he arrived at Eagle Springs.

After resting for a week, Peacock undertook a search for Victorio's hidden cave. He rode up and down the trail several times in the area described by Juanita but had difficulty interpreting the landmarks. Unfortunately, there were several places along the trail that matched her descriptions.

For days, Peacock searched but was unable to locate the cave. He was aware of the Apaches' skill at camouflaging a cave or mine entrance to match the surrounding environment, but he always felt that he was on the verge of making a discovery. Weeks passed, and still he was unsuccessful. Soon, he had exhausted his supplies and was forced to seek employment, so he returned to his old job with the stage line. When he was able to arrange for the time, he would resume his search for the cave, but he was growing more and more discouraged.

Eventually, Peacock saved enough money to purchase a small ranch a short distance north of the Eagle Mountains. He kept his job with the stage line and worked the ranch in his time off. Between his job and maintaining the ranch, he had little time to continue his search for the lost cave of gold.

In 1880, Peacock was riding with a company of Texas Rangers under the commands of Lieutenant George W. Baylor and another lieutenant named North. They were responsible for patrolling the area and keeping a watch out for Victorio and his men, who had been conducting raids nearby. A message was received that the Apaches had been located at their stronghold in the Tres Castillos Mountains by Mexican soldiers led by General Joaquin Terrazas. The rangers crossed the Rio Grande to go to the aid of the Mexicans.

By the time the ranger company arrived, the Apaches had been routed and Victorio was dead. Terrazas credited one of his marksmen with bringing down the famous Apache chieftain, but the surviving Indians claimed Victorio took his own life rather than be captured.

During the fight with the Mexicans, 12 of Victorio's warriors, along with some of the tribe's women and children, managed to escape. When last seen, they were riding toward the Eagle Mountains. The rangers took pursuit.

Three days later, the rangers caught up with the fleeing Apaches in the mountains. The Indians were able to withstand the rangers' fierce charges for a while but eventually ran out of food and ammunition. They made a break during the night and fled northward for the security of the Sierra Diablo Mountains north of Van Horn, Texas. They had just entered the mountains when the band was overtaken by the rangers and every member was killed. Peacock searched the faces of the dead women for Juanita, but she was not among them. This fight marked the end of the Apache trouble in West Texas.

Years passed, and Joe Peacock, having grown older and more infirm, returned to his ranch. At intervals, he would take up his search for Victorio's cave of gold in the Eagle Mountains, but in time he was unable to make the trip.

In 1895, Peacock met Race Compton. Compton was passing through the town of Van Horn on his way to the Eagle Mountains with the intention of doing some prospecting. The two men struck up an instant friendship and learned that they shared an interest in gold. Peacock told Compton the story of Victorio's treasure and his own search for it, and for the next several years the two worked together to try to locate the cave. They remained partners for 15 years.

In 1910, Joe Peacock passed away from a lingering case of pneumonia. Compton stayed on at the Peacock ranch and continued his search for Victorio's cave. From time to time, Compton would hitchhike throughout West Texas in search of work in order to earn money to purchase supplies. He would return to the mountains and remain until his food ran out. It was during one of those trips to El Paso to look for work and purchase some dynamite that Compton was picked up for vagrancy by the sheriff and eventually introduced to Myrtle Love.

Compton confided in Love that, as soon as they let him out of the county jail, he was going to return to the Eagle Mountains with the dynamite. He confided that he had finally located Victorio's cave and that it was approximately five miles west of Eagle Springs and on the south side of the old Indian trail, a full day's horseback ride from Sierra Blanca and a half-day's ride out of Indian Hot Springs. Compton told Miss Love that recent heavy rains in the area had washed away a lot of the debris the Apaches had used to conceal the entrance to the cave. All that remained, he said, was to blast away the large rocks blocking the entrance.

The next morning, Compton was released from the county jail and given a ride to the city limits. He was last seen hitchhiking toward Sierra Blanca with a canvas pack filled with dynamite.

Miss Love never heard from Race Compton again. Was he successful in opening Victorio's long hidden cave? Did he find the gold that was reputed to have been cached there? Perhaps not. It has been suggested that Compton never made it back to the Eagle Mountains. An old timer who lived in Sierra Blanca had known Compton. He said an old man who was never formally identified had died of a heart attack while hitchhiking on the highway from El Paso to Sierra Blanca. His body had been found on the side of the road early one morning, his head lying atop the pack of dynamite that was to open the cache of riches for which he had searched for so many years. The dead man was given a pauper's burial in Sierra Blanca. Though he never saw the corpse, the Sierra Blanca resident was certain the dead man was Race Compton.

Today there's a historical marker at Eagle Springs where the old stagecoach station used to be located. Aside from a few deer hunters, few people ever enter the harsh and forbidding realm of the Eagle Mountains. The area is far from well-traveled roads and much of it is inaccessible. Most of those who are familiar with the story of Chief Victorio's cave of gold insist that the treasure is still there.

Chapter 20

Curly Bill Brocius and the Skeleton Canyon Treasure

Though never garnering the notoriety and headlines of more famous outlaws such as Billy the Kid, Jesse James, Butch Cassidy, Belle Starr, and others, Curly Bill Brocius was nonetheless one of the most colorful and dangerous outlaws ever to occupy the American Southwest

Brocius was a cattle rustler and gunman who plied his trade for the most part in and around the town of Tombstone, Cochise County, Arizona Territory.

It is believed that Brocius was born in 1845, and most researchers name Crawfordsville, Indiana, as his birthplace, although Missouri has also been cited as his origin. At least one account states that his real name was William B. Graham. The outlaw's name has afforded some controversy, and Brocius may be an alias. It is occasionally spelled "Brocious" in some accounts. Other evidence suggests that he may be William "Curly Bill" Bresnaham, who was convicted of attempted robbery and murder in El Paso, Texas, in 1878.

For a time Brocius served as a tax collector for Cochise County Sheriff Johnny Behan. Part of his job was to make cattle rustlers pay taxes on their stolen cattle, the proceeds of which paid Brocius's salary.

Descriptions of Brocius's behavior paint him as often drunk and always mean. He was regarded as a deadly pistol shot who could allegedly pick off a running jackrabbit and shoot the quarters from between the fingers of men he forced to serve as volunteers. Brocius was the recipient of at least two gunshot wounds, and it is believed that he killed at least a dozen men, including having a role in the assassination of Morgan Earp, the lawman brother of Wyatt Earp.

History records that Brocius was killed on March 24, 1882. A posse led by Wyatt Earp came upon Brocius and eight additional gang members encamped near the edge of a wash associated with Iron Springs in Arizona's Whetstone Mountains. During the ensuing gunfight, according to Earp biographers, Wyatt shot Brocius in the chest with a load of buckshot, killing him instantly. That account came from Earp himself.

However, Earp's version of what occurred is in dispute. Author Steve Gatto cites evidence that Brocius was not even in Arizona at the time of the shootout at Iron Springs. There are reports that Brocius was in El Paso, Texas, during the time of the gunfight.

The lives of most noted outlaws are sometimes a mix of legend and truth. Brocius is no exception, and one of the most intriguing legends has the outlaw reappearing nearly a decade after his alleged death at the hands of Wyatt Earp. The same legend describes his role in a robbery that yielded a fortune in gold and silver coins, golden church artifacts, and diamonds – a treasure worth millions.

For a time, a gang of bandits led by Curly Bill Brocius attacked and robbed stagecoaches and travelers in the vicinity of Silver City, New Mexico. By the time the spoils of their robberies had been divided by the five men, the rewards seemed insufficient given the risks. Brocius wanted to move on to bigger, more lucrative targets.

One evening, Brocius, along with his fellow outlaws Jim Hughes, Zwing Hunt, Billy Grounds, and Doc Neal, met to discuss some new opportunities. Several years earlier, Hughes had killed three people during a stagecoach robbery in Texas. He had been pursued and nearly captured by law enforcement authorities, but succeeded in escaping across the border into Mexico. He fled to Monterrey, where he lived for a year. During his time there, Hughes grew proficient in the Spanish language and also learned of the various riches to be found in that city.

When Hughes decided to leave Monterrey, he traveled westward and ended up in the Mexican state of Sonora. There, he fell in with Jose Estrada, a feared Mexican bandit and killer. Hughes proved to be a hardworking and useful member of the gang – one of 30 men. He remained with Estrada for several months. Following a series of raids, the Estrada gang was pursued by an army patrol, forcing them to take refuge in the Sierra Madres, not far from the border with the United States. At that point, Hughes bade his friend goodbye and told him that he was going to go back to Texas. A short time later, Hughes joined Curly Bill's gang.

While Hughes was meeting with Brocius and other members of the gang that evening in Silver City, he related stories of his time in Mexico, and in particular, Monterrey. Impressed, Curly Bill suggested that they travel to the city and raid it. All agreed, eager for the wealth they knew they would realize from such an escapade.

Hughes thought the idea a good one, but warned that a gang of Anglos riding into the city would arouse suspicion. Besides, he said, five men were not enough; they needed a small army. He came up with an idea. He would contact his friend Estrada and enlist his aid in conducting the raid. He would tell the Mexican bandit that disposing of the loot in Mexico would be a problem, and that if he transported it to the United States, he and Brocius would arrange for its exchange, converting it into cash and making him and all of his gang members rich men. Hughes had a plan, and it involved double-crossing the greedy Estrada.

Hughes said he would accompany Estrada and his men to Monterrey. After the raid, he would lead them back to the United States to a specific location. Once Estrada's gang and all of the loot were within the confines of a seldom-traveled canyon located in southeastern Arizona, explained Hughes, Brocius and his gang would ambush them and take the treasure. Hughes's plan appealed to Brocius and the other gang members, and they agreed to send their companion into Sonora to find Estrada.

After weeks of planning and travel, the raid was ready to be launched. Telegraph wires leading into Monterrey were cut. Mules were procured to transport the booty. On entering the town, the gang robbed the bank and ransacked the church. During the raid, four Monterrey police officers were shot and killed, along with at least one dozen soldiers. Three hours later, the band rode out of town with gold and silver bars and coins, priceless golden statuary from the church, and, to their amazement, a fortune in diamonds that had been stored in the bank's vaults. All of the loot was packed onto the mules.

The outlaws fled due west, following the wagon road to Torreon. Occasional gunfights erupted with pursuers, who eventually turned back. Near Torreon, the party turned northward and made their way along a snaking road through the Sierra Madres that eventually took them to an old smugglers' trail that led into Arizona.

Once across the border, Hughes, Estrada, and the rest of the weary bandits made camp in a narrow canyon near the confluence of what are now Skeleton Creek and South Fork Skeleton Creek. By this time, most of Estrada's gang members had been paid off and sent home. The treasure was now guarded by the leader himself, along with a dozen hand-picked men. Hughes told Estrada he was going to ride ahead and make the arrangements for the transfer of the treasure and would return in a few days.

Several days later, Hughes returned to the canyon with Grounds, Hunt, and Neal. For reasons not clear, Brocius, the acknowledged leader of the gang, remained in Silver City. Early one morning, Hughes led his partners to a point about two miles north of Estrada's camp, where they set up an ambush. At that location, the canyon was so narrow that the mules and riders would have to pass through single-file and the Mexicans would be easy targets. When the outlaws were positioned for the assault, Hughes told them to open fire at his signal, which would be a pistol shot. This done, he rode back to Estrada's camp.

Hours later, Estrada and his men loaded the treasure onto the mules and doused the campfires. The riders mounted and prepared for travel. Hughes told Estrada they were to ride to Silver City, where the treasure would be exchanged for cash. Following the transfer, he said, there would be a celebration. By the time the treasure caravan entered the narrow part of the canyon, it was late afternoon. Hughes was in the lead, with Estrada riding behind him.

When the line of riders and pack animals was strung out in the narrow defile, Hughes, riding in the lead, turned in his saddle and shot Estrada in the head. At this, Grounds, Hunt, and Neal opened fire with their rifles. Within seconds, all of the Mexicans were dead.

During the slaughter, the pack mules that were carrying a portion of the treasure panicked and bolted. Unable to overtake and control them, the outlaws decided that the only way to stop them was to shoot them. All but two were downed before they could escape from the canyon. One was shot just outside of the canyon entrance, and the last was finally overtaken miles away near Geronimo's Peak.

With the killing of the mules, a problem arose: There was no way to transport the greatest portion of the Monterrey loot to the designated hiding place. Neal volunteered to ride to Silver City and secure more mules. Grounds and Hunt would remain in the canyon to guard the treasure. While discussion ensued, Hunt asked why Brocius was to get a share of the treasure when he had done nothing to help obtain it. Eventually it was decided that Hughes would ride back to Silver City and tell Brocius that Estrada had escaped with the treasure. If Brocius acted suspicious, Hughes would simply kill him. Hughes would then return with the necessary mules and transport the treasure to a safe location.

Within hours after Hughes rode away, Grounds, Hunt, and Neal decided to keep the treasure for themselves. With

Brocius and Hughes nowhere around, they could divide the fortune three ways instead of five. Doc Neal was elected to travel to a nearby ranch and purchase some oxen to carry the treasure. Taking a pocketful of the gold coins, he set out on his mission. In the meantime, Grounds and Hunt set up a campsite.

Once Neal was out of sight, Grounds and Hunt gathered up the treasure that had been carried by the mules, excavated a deep hole not far from the massacre site, and buried most of it. According to some estimates, the two men buried, in 1890s values, approximately $80,000 worth of the loot. Some researchers quibble with this figure, claiming it could have been as much as $1 million.

Neal rode into camp two days later, leading four oxen roped together. It did not take him long to realize he had been double-crossed by his two partners. He noted that several of the leather pouches containing the treasure lay open and empty, and several of the mule packs were missing. He said nothing, fearing that manifesting his suspicions might get him killed. The following morning, the three men loaded the remaining treasure onto the oxen.

For the next two days, the outlaws herded the slow-moving oxen northeastward toward New Mexico. Just before reaching the border, they turned northward into the Peloncillo Mountains. As they rode along, Neal noted that Grounds and Hunt often rode close together and spoke in whispers. Neal was convinced that the two men intended to kill him. At the first opportunity he broke away from the pack train and fled eastward. He later reported that Grounds and Hunt fired their rifles at him as he fled, but he was not struck.

Neal rode straight for Silver City. There, he discovered Brocius had been arrested for fighting and was in the jailhouse. Hughes had taken up residence in Brocius's cabin. Hughes had not seen Brocius since his return and had been unable to tell him of the concocted story of Estrada's escape with the treasure. When Neal told Hughes all that had transpired after he left the canyon, he grew angry. The two men decided that when Brocius was released from jail, the three of them would go after Grounds and Hunt.

When Brocius was finally released, Hughes and Neal took him to a saloon, where they explained all that had transpired. Brocius was livid. At one point, a young barmaid banged into his chair, and the always-volatile Brocius, losing control, pulled his revolver and shot her dead. Realizing they were facing a serious charge of murder, the three men fled Silver City with a posse at their heels.

Forty miles later, according to one account, the posse caught up with the three outlaws at the little town of Shakespeare, to the southwest, and cornered them. During the ensuing gunfight, Neal was killed. Brocius and Hughes were forced to surrender and within hours were hanged in the dining room of Shakespeare's Pioneer Hotel.

By the time Brocius and Hughes were dangling from the rafters of the Pioneer, Hunt and Grounds, after filling their pockets with gold coins from the Monterrey hoard, had buried the remainder of the treasure in a canyon running out of the Davis Mountains near Morenci, Arizona. After this, they rode to Tombstone.

Within weeks, word of the massacre of Estrada and his gang members in Skeleton Canyon circulated throughout much of the Southwest, but no one save Grounds and Hunt knew the circumstances. While maintaining their secret, the two men spent their gold recklessly in Tombstone.

Grounds remembered a former girlfriend living in

Charleston, a small town not far from Tombstone, and he went to see her. Since Grounds had left her months earlier, she had taken up with the Charleston butcher. When Grounds arrived and showed her his gold coins, she decided to go back to him. One night, as they were lying together in bed, he told her the story of the Monterrey raid, the treasure, and the incident in Skeleton Canyon. The next morning after Grounds returned to Tombstone, the woman told the butcher what she had learned. The butcher rode to Tombstone to inform the sheriff, Bill Breckenridge, about the two murderers, Grounds and Hunt, living in his town. While the butcher was talking to Breckenridge, Grounds had returned to Charleston. The girlfriend immediately confessed to him what she had done. Panicked, Grounds rode his horse back to Tombstone at a hard gallop and told Hunt what had happened and the two fled.

Before departing Tombstone, Grounds took a few minutes to write a letter to his mother, who was living in San Antonio, Texas. In the letter, he told her he was coming home and that he was tired of "this wild life." He wrote that he had buried $80,000 that "I came by honestly." He said he intended to purchase a ranch near San Antonio where his mother could live out her days. Enclosed with the letter was a map showing the location of the treasure buried in Skeleton Canyon.

Grounds and Hunt detected no immediate pursuit, and they spent the first night of their flight at a ranch owned by a man named Chandler. The ranch was located 10 miles from Tombstone. The following morning, the two outlaws were awakened by Sheriff Breckenridge, who called out for them to come out of the bunkhouse with their hands up. Breckenridge, accompanied by two deputies named Gillespie and Young, had followed Grounds and Hunt from Tombstone.

Not wishing to be captured, Grounds and Hunt dashed out of the bunkhouse, firing their revolvers. Gillespie was killed immediately, and Young was incapacitated from a bullet in his leg. Breckenridge raised his shotgun and discharged it, the pellets striking Grounds in the head. Dropping the shotgun, the sheriff pulled his revolver and shot Hunt in the chest. The two wounded outlaws were tossed into a wagon appropriated from rancher Chandler and transported back to Tombstone. Grounds died before arriving and Hunt was rushed to the local hospital. On first examination, the doctor gave him no chance to live.

Hunt lingered on, however. He requested that the authorities contact his brother Hugh. Days later, Hugh arrived from Tucson. The two men visited for only a few minutes before Hugh left. That afternoon, Hugh leased a horse and buggy, clandestinely removed his brother from the hospital, and drove out of town. The escape was not discovered until the next day.

On a hunch, Sheriff Breckenridge determined that the Hunt brothers were on their way to Skeleton Canyon to dig up the treasure. He assembled a small posse and headed in that direction. Several miles from the massacre site, Breckenridge encountered a freshly dug grave next to an oak tree. On the trunk of the tree, the name Zwing Hunt was carved. Breckenridge ordered his deputies to dig up the grave to make certain. Only a few inches below the surface they found Hunt's body. It was reburied, and the posse returned to Tombstone. Before leaving, Breckenridge and his men examined the area closely but found no evidence of additional digging for the treasure. With the death of Zwing Hunt, all of the participants in the caching of the Monterrey treasure were dead.

The letter and map that Grounds had sent to his mother in San Antonio are still in the possession of the descendants. Both are reported to be in good condition, and the map supposedly provides clear directions to the location of the buried treasure. To date, however, no attempt has been made by the family to locate and recover the cache. Furthermore, they have resisted all attempts by others to examine letter and map.

Over the years, many have gone in search of the buried Monterrey loot, popularly known as the "Skeleton Canyon Treasure." In the canyon, dozens, perhaps hundreds, of gold and silver coins have been found, likely those scattered when the pack mules were fleeing the site of the massacre. It has been written that just before he died, Zwing Hunt wrote a description of the cache site of the remainder of the treasure that was carried away on the oxen – the portion of the treasure allegedly buried in the Davis Mountains near Morenci, Arizona.

If located today, the portion of the Monterrey loot buried in Skeleton Canyon could be worth as much as $20 million, according to some estimates. Regarding the parcel of the treasure that was transported out of Skeleton Canyon and later buried by Grounds and Hunt in what was referred to as the Davis Mountains, an examination of topographic maps shows no such mountain range in the area, although there is a Davis Mountain.

While exploring a canyon associated with this Davis Mountain in 1991, a man who had been searching for the treasure encountered some curious evidence of it. He chanced across a part of a canyon where he saw enough to convince him that something large had been buried there. Nearby, he also found the remains of oxen. Suspecting this might be the cache of the remaining Skeleton Canyon treasure, the man made plans to return with appropriate digging tools and excavate. Unfortunately, he suffered a heart attack a week later and was never able to undertake another trip to the canyon.

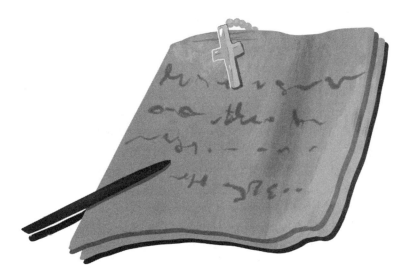

Chapter 21

Chato's Treasure

Though few people have ever heard of him, Pedro "Chato" Nevarez may have been the most notorious and successful bandit in American history. He lived in an era of the American southwest when there were not many newspapers; thus his outlaw exploits went unrecorded, for the most part. Over the years since his passing, Nevarez's life has evolved into a mixture of legend, lore, and fact, and save for his 10-year career as a fearsome, bloodthirsty highwayman, very little is known about him.

A handful of researchers believe Nevarez (his name is sometimes seen as Narvaiz in the literature) was an Indian, possibly Apache, but little evidence exists to support this notion. Some have claimed that he was Mexican, and still others insist he was the offspring of an Apache father and a Mexican mother. He was given the name Pedro at birth, but soon acquired the nickname "Chato," which is Spanish slang for "snub-nose" or "cut nose." According to one of the legends that surround Nevarez, he lost a portion of his nose during a knife fight.

Nevarez is perhaps New Mexico's earliest known outlaw, the leader of a gang of brigands and cutthroats active during the early to middle of the seventeenth century that preyed upon wagon trains and travelers making their way up and down the Rio Grande valley that bisected north–south the southern part of the state. Chato's gang consisted of Apache and Pueblo Indians along with some Mexicans. Between 1639 and 1649, it was generally acknowledged that no one was safe along the well-traveled roads that paralleled the Rio Grande near present-day Las Cruces, New Mexico. Not only did Nevarez and his men relieve their victims of their money and gold, they occasionally took prisoners with them back to their hideout and subjected them to slow and sadistic torture.

Favorite targets of Nevarez and his gang were the caravans and pack trains coming out of Mexico carrying supplies to the Spanish settlements up and down the river and traveling as far north as Santa Fe. The caravans routinely transported food, guns, ammunition, mining equipment, and occasionally gold and silver for barter. The pack trains were seldom accompanied by guards or a military escort, thus rendering them vulnerable to attack. Following each raid on a supply train, Nevarez and his gang would return to their hideaway deep in a location known as Soledad Canyon in a nearby mountain range.

One of Nevarez's most successful raids took place during April 1649. From a point of concealment among some rocks, Chato and his men watched as a long, northbound pack train wound its way along the river road. The pack train was led by a contingent of monks. Months earlier, this party had departed the monastery at Alcoman, located 40 miles north of Mexico City. Packed onto the mules were quantities of chalices, crosses, cups, candleholders, and statuary, all made of gold and manufactured in Mexico City. The items were intended to be distributed among the various missions located along the Rio Grande valley.

Around sundown the monks guided the caravan into a wooded section along the banks of the river and prepared to make camp for the night. After the pack saddles had been removed from the mules and the animals turned out to graze, the monks began gathering firewood. Nevarez chose this moment to attack. Without warning, the bandit leader and his men swooped down upon the unsuspecting holy men from a nearby low ridge. The monks, members of the Augustinian order and dedicated to non-violence, were unarmed and offered no resistance.

The outlaws rounded up the mules, replaced the treasure-laden packs, and herded them away toward the east. The band halted after two miles, dismounted, and unpacked the animals in order to examine their newly acquired booty. In addition to the wealth in golden church items, Nevarez was delighted to discover dozens of pouches filled with silver coins. Chato decided to divide some of the spoils on the spot and doled out portions of the coins to his men. This done, the golden items were repacked and transported to the canyon, where they were placed in a cave.

On foot, the Augustinian monks made their way back down the trail to El Paso del Norte, a city on the Mexican side of the Rio Grande (later known as Juárez). They reported the robbery to their superiors at the mission there, and a full account of the event was forwarded to the officials at the Alcoman mission.

Weeks later, a mounted contingent of armed soldiers arrived in El Paso, all disguised as monks and leading a pack train. The train carried little of value, but to the casual observer it resembled the others that traveled the valley road to the north bearing church items and coins. The soldiers' intent was to invite an attack from Nevarez and his gang, surprise them, and attempt to capture or kill as many as possible.

When one of Chato's scouts reported the approach of the new pack train, Nevarez assembled his men and made preparations to attack it. At a selected point along the trail, the outlaws charged up and out of an arroyo and were among their intended victims within seconds. Much to the surprise and dismay of the bandits, the riders threw back their cloaks, withdrew weapons, and set upon the outlaws.

The fight lasted only minutes and several on each side were killed or wounded. The Nevarez gang, however, had been badly defeated, and those not slain were taken prisoner, roped together, and marched back to Alcoman, hundreds of miles to the south. Among the prisoners was Chato Nevarez.

Months later, Nevarez and his surviving companions were tried in Alcoman, found guilty of robbery and murder and sentenced to hang. While they awaited their fate on the gallows, the outlaws were housed in filthy, cramped, stone-walled cells. Their constant visitors were rats and cockroaches.

Aware that such things had been accomplished in the past, Nevarez decided to try to buy his way out of prison. Over a period of time, the outlaw befriended one of the guards as well as the monk who accompanied him when food was brought to the prisoners. Chato told the guard many stories of the huge cache of gold and other riches far to the north in Soledad Canyon. When Nevarez described the treasure and its location to the guard, the monk, unknown to the other two men, wrote the information down. Despite his efforts to purchase his freedom, Nevarez, along with his companions, was hanged one week later.

The life and times of the outlaw Chato Nevarez would likely be relegated to a mere footnote in New Mexican and southwestern history were it not for an unusual event that occurred in 1930. In July of that year, a man wrestled a very old, heavy metal safe into an El Paso establishment that specialized in refurbishing and repairing such items, along with old trunks, chests, and strongboxes. The owner of the safe explained to the proprietor that the item had come from the old monastery in Alcoman and had been handed down in his family for a number of generations. He left the safe to be restored and made usable.

Days later, as he was removing a rusted section of an interior wall of the safe, the proprietor discovered an old document that had apparently been hidden between the inner lining and the outer wall. The document, in longhand, was written in Castilian Spanish and was somewhat beyond the grasp of the proprietor or any of his employees. When the owner of the safe returned, he was given the manuscript along with an explanation of the discovery.

Curious about the contents of the document, the owner of the safe sent it to a Spanish linguist at the University of Texas at Austin, who translated it into English. It turned out to be description of Chato Nevarez' treasure cave believed to be deep in the Organ Mountains near Las Cruces, New Mexico, as it was written down nearly three centuries earlier.

The translation in its exact wording reads:

Go to El Paso el Norte and inquire where the Organ Mountains are. The mountains are located up the river two days' travel from El Paso del Norte by horseback. It is a large mountain range with some peaks on it. You will find in these mountains two gaps. One is called Tortuga and the other is called Soledad. Before entering the first gap turn to your right and go to about the middle of the slope of the mountain where you will find a very thick juniper tree. From this tree proceed downhill 100 paces to a spot covered with small stones. Look for a blue stone a great deal larger than the others. A cross was made on this stone by a chisel. Remove this slab and dig about a man's height and you will find a hole full of silver taken from the packs of six mules. You will find at the bottom of this hole some boards. Remove the boards and you will find coins from three mule trains we captured and buried there. Following this go to Soledad Canyon and follow up the pass until you reach a very large spring which is the source of the water that runs through the canyon. The spring is covered with cattails.

Proceed to the right to about the middle of the slope of the mountains. Look with great care for three juniper trees which are very thick and set not very far apart. In front of these trees are a small precipice in which can be found a large flat rock on which a cross has been carved with a chisel. Between the trees and the rock exists a mine which belonged to a wealthy Spaniard named Jose Colón. The mine is so rich that the silver ore can be cut with a knife. The opening of the mine is covered by a large door we constructed from the timbers of the juniper. On top of this door is placed a large red rock. It will take 25 men to remove this rock. Just inside the door can be found gold crucifixes, images, platters, vases, and other items. Passing this, continue down into the mine shaft and you will encounter a tall stack of silver bars. Beyond this lies mining equipment. Thousands of families will be benefitted by this wealth.

Two years after the translation of the document, another one, containing the description and location of the treasure hidden by Nevarez, was discovered. It has been concluded that during the surprise attack on Nevarez and his gang, one of the outlaws managed to escape and hide among the cattails along the bank of the river. Badly wounded and losing blood, the bandit managed to crawl away. Two days later, he was found lying, near death, on the steps of the Doña Ana Mission.

Barely clinging to life, the outlaw made his final confession to the priest who attended him. He told the holy man about stealing the golden church items and described where they were hidden in Soledad Canyon. The priest wrote down the words of the dying man as he spoke, careful to include as many details as possible. The following morning, the outlaw was found dead. The priest, viewing the tale of the buried treasure as the incoherent ravings of a dying man, disregarded it and filed it along with other mission paperwork and documents. Other church duties kept the priest busy and he eventually forgot about the incident.

In October 1879, the Doña Ana Mission was attacked by the Apache war chief Victorio and his band. After killing a number of priests, monks, and Mexican laborers, the Indians ransacked the church, taking the gold and silver icons. Additionally, they raided the nearby storehouses and stole food, guns, and ammunition. Books, letters, and church documents that were encountered were simply scattered and tossed, many of them carried away by the unceasing desert winds.

Among the few documents recovered the following day was the account of the dying outlaw as it had been written down by the priest. In part it read:

In Soledad Canyon there is a natural cave in the brow of a hill opening toward the south. There is a cross cut into the rock above the entrance to the cave and directly in front of a young juniper tree. For better directions there are three medium-sized peaks toward the rising sun whose shadows converge in the morning 250 paces east of the cave entrance and a little to the south. Two hundred and fifty paces from this point directly north can be found an embankment from where by looking straight ahead you can see the Jornada del Muerto as far as the eye can see. The distance from this point to the cave should be exactly the same as the distance to the place where the shadows of the peaks converge. One hundred paces from the entrance to the cave down the arroyo you will find a dripping spring. The entrance to the cave has been covered to the depth of a man's height, and ten paces beyond the entrance there is an adobe wall which must be torn down in order to gain access. At the bottom of a long tunnel, the cave separates into two parts. The left cave contains two mule-loads worth of coined silver and the right cave contains candlesticks, images, and crucifixes taken in a robbery.

One day during the autumn of 1913, a sometime miner named Ben Brown was hunting for deer in a remote canyon in a New Mexico mountain range when he made a most serendipitous discovery. Brown spotted a deer browsing among some low-growing shrubs, aimed his rifle, and fired a shot. Unfortunately, Brown only wounded the animal, which bounded away among the rocks. Brown followed the blood-spattered trail for about 300 yards before finally losing it. Exhausted, he sat down in the shade of a large juniper tree to catch his breath. As he rested beneath the tree, he scanned the slope below him in hope of finding the wounded deer but spotted something more interesting.

Not too far distant and on the same hillside where Brown reclined, he saw an area that appeared unnatural – one that seemed to have been filled in with rocks. Based on Brown's career as a miner, he recognized immediately that the placement of the rocks was done by people, not nature. Curious, he wondered why anyone would go to so much trouble to relocate tons of rock.

Brown made his way down to the site and looked around. As he did so, he recalled the old tale so often told in the area about the outlaw Chato Nevarez burying a great treasure somewhere in Soledad Canyon. Looking around, Brown noted the three medium-sized peaks alluded to in the dying outlaw's account to the priest. From the juniper under which Brown had sat, he paced off 250 steps in the direction of the rising sun, then north for the same distance. When he stopped, he found himself on a low ridge from which he had a grand view of the Jornada del Muerto, the so-called "Journey of the Dead" or "Route of the Dead," a vast, arid plain that extended as far as the eye could see and that had claimed the lives of so many travelers in the past. Returning to the juniper tree, Brown paced off 100 steps downhill and stopped in an arroyo where the outlaw had said that a dripping spring was located. Though he searched for several minutes, he could find no evidence of one. Intuitively, however, he dug into the soft sand that composed the floor of the arroyo and found water seeping in from only eight inches below.

Early the next morning before sunrise, Brown returned to the canyon with an armload of digging tools. He found a comfortable position among the rocks and waited as the sun rose over the peaks behind him. As it did, he watched the progress of shadows across the landscape before him, and around mid-morning he noted the spot where the shadows of the three peaks converged. He walked to the location and marked it with a cairn of rocks. From this point he walked 250 paces to the west. Here, he found what he was convinced was tons of rock brought in from an adjacent slope to fill a cave. Based on what he recalled from the legend of Chato's treasure, Brown was beginning to believe he had found where it was hidden.

Over the next several days, Brown undertook the task of removing the rock fill from the vertical entrance to the cave. Working alone, he hauled away tons of debris, exposing the opening of a cave. By the time he had removed six feet of the rock, he found himself standing on a large flat stone, one that had clearly been wedged into its present position by people. Scraping away dust and gravel, Brown exposed the image of a crucifix on the surface of the stone; it had been scratched onto the rock with a chisel.

Brown was discouraged by the slow progress he was making and the grueling work involved with the excavation. He covered the flat rock with brush and debris and returned to his home in Las Cruces. The following morning, he walked into the county clerk's office and filed a mining claim on the location in Soledad Canyon. From there, he drove to a hardware store and purchased a pickup load of camping gear and more digging tools and returned to the cave. He drove as close as he could to the excavation site. Making several trips, he carried his gear the rest of the way and set up a temporary camp. He cut down what he considered to be the identifying juniper tree in case anybody else might be searching for the lost treasure of the outlaw Chato Nevarez.

Though it took most of two days Brown, wielding a heavy sledgehammer, broke up the stone bearing the image of a crucifix and removed the pieces. To his frustration, he discovered that the cave below the stone had also been filled in with rock and soil.

For the next two weeks, Brown lowered himself into the slowly deepening excavation, removing the fill one bucketful at a time. When he reached a depth of 12 feet, he observed that the shaft gradually began leveling out. It was also much narrower than the entrance, forcing Brown to crawl on his hands and knees. More time passed, and several more tons of rock and debris were removed. Just as Brown was beginning to think the project was becoming hopeless, he found a gold Spanish coin lying on the floor of the cave. It bore a date of 1635. The discovery provided Brown with a reason to continue.

Brown finally came to the adobe wall he recalled from the legend. Wielding a heavy crowbar in a cramped space, he succeeded in tearing it down. Beyond, Brown found the cave was clear for another 10 yards. He crawled through the space and came to a chamber large enough for him to stand upright. Beyond the chamber and in the light of his torch, he saw that the cave continued. He hurried over to it and was disappointed to see that at this point it, too, had been filled with gravel and soil.

The patient Brown continued with the excavation of the cave. One day, he dug out an ancient pickaxe from the debris. Later, he shipped it to an acquaintance who worked at the Chicago Field Museum of Natural History and requested an identification. Brown subsequently learned that the tool was made from hand-forged metal and the casting process suggested that it had probably been manufactured in Spain sometime during the sixteenth century. Heartened, Brown continued his backbreaking labor in the cave.

From time to time, Brown was forced to abandon the treasure site to look in on his other mining operations in widely separated locations in the region. He also began taking a week off from the heavy labor now and then to rest his aching body. For over a year, he continued the slow, painstaking process of removing the dirt fill from the cave one bucketful at a time. Weeks would pass and he would grow discouraged, only to find another artifact among the debris that would give him hope that the treasure was not far beyond.

Brown's difficulties were to grow worse. His other mines were not particularly productive, and he began losing money. Eventually he was forced to close down those operations and take jobs in and around Las Cruces in order to provide an income for himself and his family. For several years while he worked off and on in the cave, Brown was employed at other mining operations and sometimes worked as a forest ranger.

Twenty years elapsed, and Brown was still excavating rock and dirt from the cave. At one point during his work, he sought some advice from a professor named Arturo Campa, who taught at the University of Denver and was regarded as an authority on tales and legends of lost treasure in the New Mexican southwest. As it turned out, Campa was keenly interested in the life and times of Chato Nevarez. Brown told Campa of his discovery and his two decades-long attempts to remove the fill from the cave. Much to Campa's surprise, Brown told him that the cave was not in the Soledad Canyon of the Organ Mountains but in a canyon of the same name in the Doña Ana range 15 miles to the west. Brown took Campa to the site.

Campa examined the excavation and was shown the point where the cave split into a Y. Brown also showed Campa all of the surface landmarks, along with the artifacts he had found in the tunnel during the previous months of digging. He explained to Campa that he was trying to obtain financial backing in order to purchase some expensive equipment that would facilitate the excavation process. Though he approached a number of potential investors, he was never able to secure the money he needed. Around the same time, several other mines he had an interest in were growing more productive, were making a profit, and required his attention. He spent less and less time at the cave.

One day, two years after Campa had visited the cave, he received a letter from Brown – one that conveyed a great deal of excitement relative to the excavation project. Brown invited Campa back to the site to show him what he had recently discovered. Because of a number of university obligations, Campa was not free to travel. Four months later, he learned that Ben Brown had died.

Brown never left a map showing the location of the cave. Furthermore, he apparently never told his wife or children of his discovery. As far as is known, the only person he shared information about the cave with was Professor Campa, who also passed away a short time later.

What was it that Brown was excited about and wanted to show Campa? Had he finally broken through the last of the rock and debris and come upon the treasure of church artifacts and silver coins? Whatever the truth regarding the treasure cave of Chato Nevarez, Ben Brown carried it with him to his grave.

Chapter 22

The Lost Train Robbery Loot of Duke Sherman

The year 1877 was a pivotal one for young Duke Sherman. It was the year he decided to turn outlaw and rob a train. For his first attempt at such a crime, it was a stunning success, for he escaped with $60,000 worth of gold. It was also a spectacular failure, in that it cost Sherman his life.

Eighteen-year old Duke Sherman had grown weary of his job of mucking out stables and feedlots at the Omaha, Nebraska, stockyards. The days were long, the work hard, and the money was barely enough to keep him alive. While his friends went to town to drink and gamble, Sherman counted out what few coins he had to pay for his room and meals. To add to his frustration, the yardmaster continually harassed and harangued young Sherman, making his life miserable.

As he raked and mucked, Sherman pondered ways to change his life, to make more money.

One evening as Sherman was passing by the Omaha train depot for the Chicago, Burlington, and Quincy Railroad, he overheard a conversation between the telegrapher and an engineer named A. L. Clayburg. Clayburg was telling the telegrapher about a shipment of gold coins leaving the next morning for Lincoln, 50 miles to the southwest. The shipment, valued at $60,000, was to be delivered to the bank at Lincoln to be used to invest in property for the railroad. The gold coins were to be transported in several metal boxes.

As Sherman continued on toward his room, his mind swam with images of $60,000 worth of gold coins. If only he could get his hands on that kind of money, he would no longer have to rake out cattle pens. Before he had covered another 50 yards, Sherman had come up with a plan: He had decided that he was going to rob the train of the gold shipment. He turned around and headed straight back to the stockyards. On arriving, he stole a buckboard and a pair of horses. After hitching the horses to the vehicle, he set out toward Lincoln, following the railroad tracks. Unknown to Sherman, he was observed in the act by three men who were taking a break from their stable-cleaning duties. After Sherman drove away, the men alerted the town marshal to the theft. As the sun was coming up the next morning, a posse of a dozen deputized citizens set out in search of Sherman and the stolen buckboard and horses. In a short time, the posse picked up his trail and followed it along the railroad tracks.

Earlier that same morning, around 2:00 a.m., engineer Clayburg spotted a herd of cattle milling about the tracks four miles out of Lincoln. Reducing the speed of the train, he blew the whistle, hoping to frighten the animals from the train's path. Clayburg slowed the train to around 10 miles per hour as the cattle slowly dispersed. Just as he was about the pick up the speed, the engineer felt a sharp jab in his ribs. Turning, he saw a man pointing a revolver at him. The man was young and his face was partially covered by a red-checkered bandanna. Clayburg looked around for his fireman and spotted him lying on the floor of the locomotive cab, his head bleeding from a severe blow.

Sherman ordered Clayburg to stop the train. Stunned at the turn of events, the engineer stood silent and still, gaping at the masked intruder. Impatient, Sherman cracked Clayburg across the head with his handgun, knocking him to the floor. A moment later, Sherman pulled the engineer to his feet and ordered him to stop the train. Clayburg, dizzy from the blow, brought the locomotive to a halt.

At gunpoint, Sherman ordered Clayburg out of the cab. On the ground, he forced the engineer to lead the way to the express car. When the train had stopped earlier, the messenger, William Lupton, had opened the door to the car to try to determine what was transpiring. He was standing in the open doorway when Sherman and Clayburg arrived. With his revolver held to Clayburg's head, Sherman ordered the messenger to throw the metal boxes containing the gold coins to the ground. The frightened messenger did as ordered. Sherman instructed the messenger to close the express car door. This done, he led Clayburg back to the locomotive and ordered him to climb into the cab and continue on to Lincoln. (One account states that Sherman was assisted by two accomplices, but this seems doubtful).

As the train pulled away, Clayburg looked out of the cab and spotted the robber driving a buckboard out from behind a grove of trees toward the boxes of gold coins. A moment later, as the train rounded a bend, Clayburg lost sight of the outlaw. Pulling the buckboard up next to the boxes, Sherman climbed out and loaded the heavy containers onto the bed. Moments later, he was whipping the horses to a fast pace as the wagon bounced along the prairie toward the northwest. Sherman intended to travel to Central City, bury his new-found fortune, and begin to make plans for a new life.

After traveling a mile, Sherman noted that the horses were growing tired. He realized that the great weight of the $60,000 worth of gold coins represented a significant load for the team. After five miles, the horses had slowed to a trot, and after another two miles they were walking, despite Sherman's trying to whip them on to greater speed.

The posse that had been following the tracks of the buckboard arrived at the scene of the train robbery. They saw indentations on the ground near the tracks where the metal boxes had been tossed and subsequently loaded into the buckboard. The posse continued to follow the tracks of the vehicle that led toward the northwest.

After crossing the Big Blue River, near the present-day town of Staplehurst, one of the horses pulled up lame. Sherman urged the team on with his whip but after another 200 yards, the animals could proceed no farther.

Sherman decided that the only way he could get the gold to Central City was to acquire a fresh pair of horses. Since he was traveling through farm and ranch country, he determined it would be an easy matter to steal them. He unhitched the weary animals from the buckboard and turned them loose to graze on the abundant prairie grasses. Before setting off in search of fresh mounts, Sherman pondered the gold in the back of the wagon. He decided it would be foolish to leave it in the open, where a passing horseman might find it. One by one, Sherman unloaded the metal boxes and carried them 20 yards from the road. After locating a flat rock, he scraped out a shallow excavation into which he placed the containers. After refilling the hole, he covered it with grass to make it look much like the rest of the prairie. This done, he set out in search of fresh horses.

Two hours later, the posse arrived at the location where Sherman had abandoned the buckboard. Not far away, they spotted the horses that Sherman had turned loose, but there was no sign of the robber, nor was there any sign of the metal boxes filled with gold coins. A deputy offered the notion that the outlaw had probably buried the gold at some location between the robbery site and the present location of the wagon.

The marshal decided to split the posse into two groups. One group was to backtrack along the trail and search for a place where the gold might have been buried. The other group would continue to search for Sherman.

Meanwhile, Sherman arrived at a farm two miles from the abandoned wagon. Seeing no one about, he made his way to the barn, where he found several horses in their stalls. As he was placing a bridle on one of the animals, Sherman was startled by the sudden appearance of the farmer. Sherman drew his revolver and fired a shot at the man, wounding him in the shoulder. The farmer turned and ran toward his house. There, he retrieved his shotgun and headed back to the barn. As he arrived, Sherman, mounted bareback, was riding the horse out of the wide doorway. The farmer raised his shotgun and emptied both barrels at the intruder, knocking Sherman off the horse.

As he lay dying in front of the barn, Sherman tried to explain to the farmer about the gold coins buried near the buckboard, but the farmer understood little of what was said. By the time the posse arrived an hour later, Duke Sherman was dead.

The ambitious and adventurous but misguided Sherman never lived to realize his dream of wealth. His corpse was transported to some lonely spot out on the prairie and buried without ceremony. A wooden marker was set up but over the years, it has long since gone the way of objects at the mercy of the winds and the rains of the area. The location of his grave has been forgotten.

The $60,000 worth of gold coins buried not far from Staplehurst have been searched for from time to time, but never found. If located today, the hoard would be worth well over half a million dollars.

Chapter 23

Mississippi Train Robbery Treasure

Duke Sherman wasn't the only outlaw who robbed a train and buried the loot only to have it lie underground un-recovered. Three enterprising Mississippi train robbers stole a large metal strongbox filled with gold coins but were forced to bury it during subsequent pursuit. None of the three lived long enough return to the cache.

During the early part of the twentieth century, northern Mississippi was given over to extensive croplands devoted to the growing of cotton. As a result of the need to transport this harvest to northern and eastern markets, and because wagon trains were slow and undependable, the need arose for a system of railroad lines linking the small communities where the cotton was delivered, ginned, and baled for trans-port.

One of the most ubiquitous railroad lines was the Illinois Central, which ran through a significant portion of Mississippi carrying passengers, freight, mail, and supplies. Occasionally, the railroad line transported payrolls of cash as well as gold and silver coins.

Charlie Bowman was employed by the Illinois Central as a member of a track repair crew working near Water Valley, a small north-central Mississippi town in Yalobusha County. On the morning of April 21, 1909, Bowman overheard a conversation between several men about a payroll consisting of gold coins that was being shipped by the railroad. The train carrying the gold was scheduled to pass down the line in a week.

Bowman was intrigued by the information, and his head swam with the possibilities of acquiring such a fortune. He decided to make plans to steal it. The following evening, he revealed his scheme to two friends – James B. Cartwright and Bob Tyson. Over the next few days, the three men reviewed their strategy for obtaining the gold shipment. One morning, they set the plan in motion by boarding the southbound Illinois Central train as passengers at Taylor, 10 miles north of Water Valley.

Sitting nervously in a passenger car with other travelers, the three waited until the train was two miles out of Taylor. At that point, one of the men rose from his seat, approached the conductor, and pointed a revolver at his head. While another of the outlaws cautioned the passengers to remain calm and stay in their seats, Bowman made his way out of the car, over the coal tender, and into the locomotive cab. Pointing his weapon at the engineer, he threatened to kill him if he did not stop the train.

Once the train was halted, the three outlaws walked to

the express car, forced open the door, and located the strongbox. It was secured with a large sturdy lock. The three
dragged the heavy object to the door and pushed it out onto
the ground next to the tracks. This done, Bowman waved his
handgun at the engineer and instructed him to continue on
to Water Valley.

Once the train was out of sight, the three bandits struggled with the weight of the strongbox. With great difficulty,
they managed to alternately carry and drag it to a nearby
bridge that crossed the tracks. Unable to break into the
strongbox and unwilling to transport it on foot any farther,
the three decided to bury it and return to reclaim it when excitement over the robbery died down. Struggling, they
dragged the strongbox to a location 100 feet west of the end
of the bridge. Here, they excavated a hole and buried it. After
refilling the hole, they noted three large oak trees near the
site of the cache and felt certain they could easily return to
the site in the future.

Tyson suggested that the three travel to Arkansas and
hide out for a time at the home of his sister who, he claimed,
would allow them to remain there for a time. On foot, the
three train robbers set off on the long journey.

When the train arrived at Water Valley a half-hour after
the robbery, the conductor notified the local law enforcement
authorities. Before another hour passed, a small posse had
been assembled and dispatched on horseback to the scene of
the crime. Because of the drag marks caused by the heavy
strongbox, the posse had little difficulty picking up the trail
of the bandits. West of the bridge they noted that the drag
marks had ceased, but the tracks of the three outlaws were
plain. They set out in pursuit, and four hours later caught
sight of Bowman, Cartwright, and Tyson.

On spotting the pursuing posse, the three train robbers drew their revolvers, took shelter behind some trees, and began firing away at the lawmen. Within minutes, Bowman and Tyson were killed and Cartwright was taken prisoner.

Under questioning, Cartwright refused to reveal where the strongbox was buried. One of the posse members recalled the drag marks made by the heavy chest and suggested that it would be an easy task to follow them and retrieve the gold. Unfortunately, a heavy rain had fallen that night and all signs of the marks had been washed away. Several members of the posse searched in the area where they remembered following the drag marks west of the bridge but found nothing.

Cartwright maintained his silence and refused to cooperate with the lawmen. He was subsequently charged with train robbery, tried, found guilty, and sentenced to 20 years in prison. Cartwright decided to serve his sentence, try for an early parole, return to the cache site, and retrieve the gold.

Cartwright's plan failed to materialize. During his 12th year of imprisonment he developed a severe case of tuberculosis and doctors gave him only a few weeks to live. Disheartened, Cartwright decided to try to salvage at least a part of his plan by letting his brother, Robert, know where the strongbox filled with gold was buried. He sent for Robert, who lived in Oxford, Mississippi.

When Robert arrived at the prison, he found his brother near death on a hospital cot. Cartwright related the particulars of the train robbery, of dragging the heavy strongbox into the woods west of the bridge, and burying it. Cartwright provided landmarks, specifically, the proximity of the three large oak trees near the cache. Two days later, James Cartwright died.

Robert Cartwright remained long enough to see to the

burial of his brother. This done, he returned to Oxford and immediately began making plans to travel to Lafayette County and search for the fortune he knew was buried near the old bridge. Arriving at the location several days later, Robert was dismayed to discover that a recent fire had destroyed the forest for miles around. The dramatic alteration of the environment left him confused, and he was unable to discern any of the landmarks described to him by this brother. He spent several hours attempting to get his bearings west of the bridge, but the large oak trees described by his brother were no longer there.

Years later, James Cartwright's story eventually became known to the public. Several searches for the buried gold were undertaken, but none were successful. The old bridge site is accessible today, located where Mississippi Highway 7 crosses the railroad tracks south of the town of Taylor. The area where the strongbox is thought to be buried is now covered with second-growth timber and a thick tangle of underbrush. Under the shade of the trees and beneath the thick brush, a fortune in gold coins lies to this day.

Chapter 24

Nate Champion's Lost Treasure

Some outlaws have been subjected to different treatment over the years, depending on the motivation, preparation, and professionalism of the writers writing about them. Nathan Champion is a good example of this. According to some who refer to themselves as historians, and who are referred to by others as "revisionists," Champion, who was called Nate, was a successful and well-respected Wyoming rancher who had the bad luck of having some relationships with lawbreakers. Champion has been described by some of these writers as one of the innocent victims of the famous Johnson County War.

Others portray Champion as no stranger to outlawry and contend that he was a participant in a number of illegal activities, including rustling livestock and murder. Rustling, it was believed, was the way rancher Champion built up his cattle herd. Around Wyoming's Johnson and Converse Counties, Champion was known among his peers "the king of rustlers." He led a gang of cattle thieves who referred to themselves as the Red Sash Gang. A number of the cattle thieves who rode with Champion's gang went on to become members of the more famous Wild Bunch, which included Butch Cassidy and the Sundance Kid.

One particularly intriguing aspect of the Nate Champion story is that he reputedly buried a large cache of gold nuggets somewhere on his property, the location of which was believed to have been lost when he was killed in a shootout with vigilantes.

It is believed that Champion purchased the KC Ranch at Powder Springs, Wyoming, with gold he earned from his rustling activities. When selling stolen cattle, Champion always insisted that the payment be made in gold coins. When this could not be accomplished, he exchanged the payment for gold at the first opportunity.

After moving onto his new property, Champion buried the bulk of his gold not far from his ranch house. The fact that he buried a quantity of gold coins has never been in question, for he stated as much to a number of acquaintances. The precise location of the cache, however, was never revealed.

For months, cattle detectives and ranchers were certain that Champion was behind the loss of cattle. He was never caught in the act of rustling, in large part because he ordered his ranch hands to do the work while he remained at a safe distance. When livestock thefts became too much to bear, the Wyoming Stock Growers Association decided to enact what was termed "the Wyoming roundup laws." These laws provided the agents of the association carte blanche to seize the herds of anyone suspected of stealing cattle. In truth, members of the association and their gangs of vigilantes, most of whom were little more than hired gunmen brought in from Texas, abused the laws and often reinterpreted them to seize livestock for themselves from ranchers they simply did not care for. These activities were the precursor for what came to be known as the Johnson County War.

The Stock Growers Association's army of mercenaries compiled a list of ranchers they intended to go after, and at the top of that list was Nate Champion. Just below Champion was his partner, Nick Rae (also spelled Ray).

The mercenaries' plan to take Champion was simple and crude: They would attack the KC Ranch by riding in and firing their weapons. They never had any intention of taking Champion alive. Unfortunately for the gunmen, the defense of the KC Ranch by Champion, Rae, and a number of ranch hands was surprisingly effective, providing time for other targeted ranchers in the area to band together to counteract the attack.

The assistance from neighbors, however, came too late for Champion. After his house was set on fire, the rancher charged out of the burning structure, firing a pair of revolvers at the gunmen. Champion was shot down, struck by 28 bullets. As he lay dying, Champion's final words, according to one account, were, "Goodbye boys, if I never see you again."

Another account stated that after Champion's death, a small notebook taken from his body was given to Sam Clover, a reporter from the Chicago Herald who had accompanied the raiders. The quote attributed to Champion and printed in the Herald was, in fact, the final entry in the notebook.

In the weeks after the assault on the KC Ranch, word spread of Champion's buried cache of gold coins. The ranch was visited by hopeful treasure hunters who dug hundreds of holes, probed the well, and turned over every stone in the pasture. They sifted through the ashes and ruins of the burned-down ranch house, but nothing was ever found.

In 1914, a stranger arrived in Johnson County and asked for directions to Champion's old KC Ranch. With curiosity getting the better of them, three local men, convinced that the newcomer was up to no good, confronted him in a local cafe and asked him about his business. The stranger admitted that he had information pertaining to the location of Champion's cache of gold and that he intended to search for it.

The local men advised the newcomer that the tale of buried treasure was likely not true and, at best, conjecture. They informed him of previous attempts to locate the gold, all of which had ended in failure. They did their best to discourage the newcomer from traveling to the KC Ranch location. At that point, the stranger extracted a folded piece of paper from his coat pocket, opened it up, and spread it out across the table. The map, he explained, purported to show the location of the buried gold and was allegedly drawn by Nate Champion himself. How the map came into his possession, he never revealed.

Concerned that he might be run out of town by the three men before he had an opportunity to search for the gold, the stranger allowed them to examine the map. He asked them for information about specific landmarks indicated on the map, such as trees, creeks, and roads. After examining the map closely, the three men decided it was probably authentic.

According to the map, the gold was cached in an abandoned well located 40 to 60 yards northeast of the old ranch house. The house, the newcomer was informed, had been burned to the ground and the site abandoned decades ago.

It was not likely, they told him, that anything was left. Surely, argued the newcomer, some evidence of a foundation could be found. During the next few hours, the three townsfolk and the newcomer agreed to join forces and search for the cache together. If found, they agreed to divide it four ways.

Two days later, the four men searched for the location of the old KC Ranch and the presumed site of Champion's house. After looking for two hours, they encountered the remains of an old rock foundation. Presuming that this was the house site, they paced off toward the northeast in hopes of finding the abandoned well. They blocked out an area of several square yards in which to conduct their search. By sundown, however, they had encountered no evidence of a well. Over the next few days, they made several more attempts to locate the cache but were unsuccessful. The stranger finally checked out of his hotel and departed, never to be seen again.

The likelihood is that the well in which Champion cached his gold coins was filled in, either by the rancher himself or as a result of natural forces. Nothing indicates how deep the well might have been, but during the time the KC Ranch was in operation, the water table was only 12 feet below the surface.

Today, the site of the old KC Ranch is private property. The lure of Nate Champion's gold cache still attracts hopeful treasure hunters to the area, but they are denied access.

Chapter 25

Clem Durkel's Train Robbery Gang

During the autumn of 1887, Clem Durkel and four of his friends were playing cards in the bunkhouse of the DHS Cattle Ranch in Judith Basin, Montana. Roundup had been completed two weeks earlier and the men found themselves with nothing to do until spring. Card games were growing boring, and the cowhands had already spent most of their wags on a few reckless nights in town several days earlier. The tedium of waiting around the DHS Ranch for the next three months until work started up again was grating on the nerves of the men as they tried to determine some form of diversion.

One evening, as they were sitting around the bunkhouse, Durkel brought up the notion of robbing a train. The idea held some appeal to the cowhands, who had had about all of the monotony that they could stand. After kicking around a few ideas, they came up with a plan to rob the St. Paul, Minneapolis, and Manitoba Railroad (SPM & M) train as it made its way northward on a brand-new railroad bed from the town of Great Falls.

In order to avoid suspicion, the cowhands left the DHS Ranch one at a time over the next few days. Finally meeting at a predesignated point outside of Great Falls, they rode alongside the railroad tracks one afternoon, searching for an ideal location from which to pull off the robbery. They settled on a site 18 miles north of Great Falls.

The novice outlaws expected to gain little more from the holdup than some amusement. Everyone knew the SPM & M carried nothing but mail and freight. On this cold day in late November, however, the train was hauling an unanticipated shipment of $50,000 in gold coins along with 25 gold ingots. It was estimated that the total value of the golden cargo was $200,000 in 1887 values.

Because the railroad track had been completed only a few weeks earlier, the engineer guided the train along slowly, cautiously, keeping an eye out for uneven rails. As the train crested a low rise, the engineer spotted several crossties piled on the tracks 100 yards distant. His first inclination was to ram the stack of ties and break through, but as the potential for derailment was high, he slowed the train and prepared to investigate. Just as the train came to a halt, five masked men charged from behind cover on horseback, each of them brandishing a revolver. One of the men leaped from his mount and into the cab of the locomotive. While he held the engineer and fireman at gunpoint, the other four raced to the express car, called out to the messenger within, and demanded that he unlock the door. The frightened messenger did as he was instructed, slid the heavy door aside, and stared into the barrels of four handguns.

The bandits ordered the messenger to turn over anything of value. They were taken by surprise when he opened the safe and produced several canvas sacks filled with gold coins. While the outlaws marveled at their incredible luck, the messenger showed them the 25 gold ingots. Hastily, the train robbers stuffed coins and ingots into saddlebags and pockets. This done, they ordered the engineer to proceed on down the track and they rode away to the northeast.

Twenty minutes after the robbery, the SPM & M train pulled into the Fort Benton station, where the engineer located a telegraph and reported the incident to the sheriff at Great Falls. The sheriff quickly assembled a posse and, loading men and horses onto the next train, rode it northward to the holdup scene.

The posse followed the tracks of the outlaws for two miles and found that they had doubled back, crossed the tracks at a point 50 yards south of the robbery scene, and proceeded toward the confluence of the Missouri and Sun Rivers. From here, the bandits had headed west toward the small settlement of Sun River, 20 miles west of Great Falls.

Meanwhile, the five train robbers were having great difficulty transporting the heavy weight of so much gold; thus their escape was slowed to a mere walk because of the burden. Arriving at Sun River, they sought to trade for fresh mounts, but no one had any to spare. Several Sun River residents noted the look of despair on the faces of the five men.

Realizing that they needed to find a place to hide and rest their tired mounts, Durkel led his companions out of Sun River and into a seldom-traveled portion of the east slope of the Rocky Mountains. They stopped near the base of Haystack Butte, built a small fire, and prepared a meal. With a freshwater spring nearby, the outlaws decided to rest at this location for two days, divide the gold, and then be on their way. They believed they had eluded any pursuers and were confident that their holdup and getaway were completely successful. While the bandits sat around their campfire and enjoyed their evening meal, they discussed what they were going to do with their newfound fortunes. At the same time, the posse had arrived at Sun River and the sheriff was questioning residents.

Nearly everyone in the small Sun River community had seen the five men riding weary horses toting heavy packs. They pointed out the direction the men had taken on leaving town, and with no difficulty the sheriff and his men, despite the fact that the sun had gone down, located and followed the tracks of the tired mounts.

The following morning, just as the train robbers were finishing breakfast, one of them walked over to the picket line to check on the horses. As he was looking after the animals, he noticed a line of riders coming over a low ridge three quarters of a mile to the southwest. At the head of the riders was a man who was obviously pointing out the tracks left by the five outlaws the previous evening. Quickly saddling their horses and loading the gold-laden saddlebags, the outlaws abandoned much of their gear and escaped into the nearby foothills.

After riding hard for four miles, the train robbers' horses grew exhausted from the weight of riders and gold. Now and again, the outlaws could see the posse closing the distance. Realizing they needed to lighten their load, the five decided to cache the gold, make their escape through the mountains, then return another day to retrieve it.

As they were searching for a suitable location in which to hide the loot, the outlaws arrived at a small mountain lake.

Looking at the shimmering waters of the lake, Durkel was seized with an idea, which he explained to his companions. Following his lead, the bandits rode their horses into the lake, pulled the sacks of gold coins and ingots out of their saddlebags, and dropped them into the cold, shallow waters. Relieved of their heavy burdens, the five men were able to make better time riding through the mountainous terrain.

When the posse arrived at the lake, they observed how the tracks of their quarry led into the water. Believing the bandits only wished to water their horses, the pursuers continued on their way, oblivious to the fortune in gold only three feet below the surface of the lake.

Clem Durkel and his friends managed to elude the posse and escape into Idaho. Fearful of returning to the lake until things cooled off and pursuit was no longer imminent, the men separated, agreeing to meet in a year, return to the area, and recover the fortune in gold.

Several months later, two members of Durkel's gang decided that robbery was an easier way to make a living than working on a cattle ranch. They tried to rob a bank in Grangeville, Idaho, and were killed during the attempt.

Another of the train robbers murdered a man during an argument in a saloon in Lewiston, Montana, and was sentenced to a life term in prison. The fourth bandit attempted to rob a stagecoach in California, was apprehended, tried, convicted, and sentenced to 20 years of hard labor.

Clem Durkel, who conducted one of the most successful train robberies in American history, decided he had had his fill of the outlaw life and went to work on a cattle ranch in southern Idaho.

Three years later, however, Durkel decided to return to the remote lake in the eastern foothills of the Montana Rockies, near Sun River, and retrieve the gold. Because there were no established trails in this unpopulated region of the range, and because Durkel remembered little of the region and its landmarks from the time of his flight from the posse, he had difficulty getting his bearings and became lost several times.

Time after time, Durkel traveled into the mountains near Haystack Butte in search of the lake, and each time, he was disappointed. Certain that great wealth still lay beneath the waters of the elusive lake, he never gave up. By 1910, 23 years after the train robbery, Durkel had narrowed his search to two remote mountain lakes, one of which he was convinced must contain the gold.

As Durkel was growing older, out of a job, and running low on funds, he abandoned his search for a time to find work. He eventually secured employment with a man named Frank Bell, the owner of a freight line that ran goods from Helena to the mining camps in the mountains. After working for Bell for a year, Durkel told his employer the story of the train robbery, the flight from the law, the fortune in gold lying at the bottom of a shallow lake in the mountains, and his unsuccessful search for it. Bell was fascinated by the tale and offered to become Durkel's partner in the search.

Selecting one of the two lakes that Durkel believed held the treasure, the men set up a camp on its shore. For two full days, they waded into the cold waters, searching and probing for the gold coins and ingots. The longer they remained in the area, the more convinced Durkel became that this was indeed the lake into which they had dumped the loot. Unfortunately, nothing was found. Discouraged, Durkel quit his job and told Bell that he was returning to Idaho. Clem Durkel was never heard from again.

Frank Bell, however, had complete faith in Durkel's story

of the train robbery and the lost gold. Bell returned to the mountains dozens of times, locating and inspecting every small lake he encountered.

One day in 1971, Bell, now an old man, walked into a bar in Great Falls and proudly displayed a gold ingot. Bell claimed he had found the ingot near one of the two lakes identified by Durkel years earlier. The ingot was subjected to an assay that reported that it was composed of 80 percent gold.

Bell explained how he came upon the ingot. He stated that he had been convinced that one of the two lakes identified by Durkel years earlier held the gold. He had set up camp near Smith Creek and spent several days in a concentrated search of the area. Finally convinced there was nothing in the larger of the two lakes, he focused his efforts on the smaller one. For half a day and far into the night, Bell searched along the shores and in the shallow water of the lake but found nothing. Finally, as dawn was breaking over a nearby ridge, he decided to return to camp and prepare breakfast.

As Bell was making his way back toward Smith Creek, he came across a previously undiscovered trail that approached the smaller lake from the north. The trail was an old one, and decades of runoff had eroded a gully 18 inches deep along portions of it. As Bell walked along part of the trail that passed close to the lake, he was distracted by the sunlight glinting from an object a few yards ahead. Picking it up, he discovered that it was a gold ingot, one no doubt taken during the train robbery 84 years earlier.

Bell later opined that in their haste to dump the gold into the lake, one of the robbers accidentally dropped one of the ingots along the trail. Encouraged by his discovery, Bell was convinced that he had found the lake in which the remainder of the loot resided. He decided to return to Great Falls, purchase some recovery equipment, and return to the lake to retrieve the gold.

Bell encountered some difficulty in procuring the necessary equipment. As a result, his return to the lake was delayed for several weeks. According to Bell's friends, given his age and his state of deteriorating health, the excitement generated by discovering the lost lake of gold generated a heart attack. About the time Bell had intended to return to the lost lake of gold, he died. He left no map of the location and he had told none of his acquaintances where it had been found.

As far as is known, the fortune in gold still lies at the bottom of the remote, shallow mountain lake not far from Great Falls on the eastern slope of the Montana Rockies. Because of the heavy weight and specific gravity of the gold, it is probable that it has sunk to some unknown depth into the bottom of the lake during the more than a century since it was deposited there. If found today, the value of the gold is estimated to be well over $2 million.

Chapter 26

Lost Bank Robbery Loot
of the Mitchell Gang

On June 9, 1882, the notorious Mitchell Gang robbed the Platte Depository and Loan Company in Saratoga, Carbon County, Wyoming. The gang made off with $68,000 in gold coins. During their flight from a pursuing posse, the outlaws hid the loot. Subsequently, all of them were killed and the gold has never been recovered.

The Mitchell Gang was organized and led by Cornelius Mitchell. Mitchell served two years as an enlisted man in the Missouri Dragoons during the Civil War. Like many others who had spent time in the Union or Confederate armies, when Mitchell mustered out, he headed west in search of new and different opportunities. On arriving in Colorado in 1880, Mitchell fell in with a company of gold miners. While they explored and prospected one mountain range after another and panned the promising-looking streams they encountered, the men experienced little success. Tired of the rough life and the constant cold, and discouraged by not finding gold, Mitchell left the group and wandered northward into Wyoming. In Cheyenne, he landed a job dealing cards at a local tavern.

Tiring of sitting at a table and playing cards with the easy marks that made up his clientele, Mitchell longed for adventure, excitement. He decided that his calling was rustling cattle and selling them.

During the next few weeks, Mitchell recruited a gang of toughs and gunmen from the Cheyenne saloons. Before long, the gang was riding up and down the region of the North Platte River Valley stealing cattle and reselling them in Colorado. After a few months, the opportunities for rustling grew exhausted, so Mitchell cast about for other ways to make a living. He found one stealing rifles and selling them to individual citizens. This, too, ran its course, and Mitchell decided that more money was to be made robbing stagecoaches. Unfortunately, the take from these jobs did not amount to enough to hold the gang together. Mitchell determined that it was time to go where he knew there was big money. It became his intention to rob the Platte Depository and Loan Company (PD & LC) in Saratoga.

Calvin Knox, the owner of the PD & LC, was one of Saratoga's community leaders and often took coffee with the mayor, the sheriff, and other politicians. Knox was proud of his bank and regularly boasted that it was "outlaw-proof." Mitchell took Knox's boast as a challenge.

Early one morning during the first week of June 1882, Mitchell, along with his second-in-command, Clay McFord, rode into Saratoga. They entered the bank under the pretense of conducting some small amount of business and while there, looked over the layout and escape routes. From the bank, they walked the streets of the town, located the sheriff's office, and learned how many deputies were employed.

While in town, Mitchell purchased a week's worth of food and supplies. Before returning to the outlaw camp, he dug a hole and cached the goods in the middle of a thick grove of cedar trees near the bank of the North Platte River. Included with the food and supplies were fishing gear and a deck of playing cards. Mitchell believed that, following the robbery of the PD & LC, it would be necessary for the gang to hide out for a time.

Mitchell was convinced that he had thought of everything. On the morning that he led his gang into town to rob the bank, however, his cache of supplies was discovered. An area rancher named Nate Woodrow was riding along the North Platte River floodplain searching for stray cattle when he entered the grove of cedar trees and spotted Mitchell's fresh excavation. Curious, Woodrow dug into the suspicious-looking site and found the cache. Woodrow determined the people behind this were likely up to no good, so after rounding up his strays, he rode into Saratoga and informed Sheriff Holcomb of his discovery.

When Woodrow arrived in town, he found the citizens stirred and excited as a result of a robbery only a few hours earlier. According to a merchant Woodrow spoke with, eight men rode into town, robbed the bank of $68,000 in gold coins, and fled before anyone save for the PD & LC employees knew what was happening. During the robbery, a teller named Robbie Childers had been wounded.

When Woodrow finally located Sheriff Holcomb, the lawman was in the process of deputizing some citizens to go in pursuit of the robbers. Woodrow attempted to speak with Holcomb but the sheriff brushed him away, telling him he was busy. After being rebuffed a second time, Woodrow placed himself squarely in front of the sheriff and told him he knew exactly where the bank robbers were hiding out. When Holcomb stopped to listen, Woodrow explained his discovery near the North Platte River. Moments later, the rancher was leading the sheriff and his posse of seven men toward the grove of cedar trees near the river.

It was evening when the lawmen topped a low rise overlooking the grove about 100 yards away. Following instructions by Holcomb, the men dismounted, drew their revolvers, and advanced on foot toward the outlaws' campsite. When they were 50 yards away, they could see the bandits seated around a campfire cooking dinner, talking, and laughing. No guards were posted.

After creeping to within 20 yards of the bank robbers, Holcomb shouted for them to drop their guns and raise their hands. In response, Mitchell and his men drew their weapons and fired into the ranks of the lawmen. During the shootout that followed, all of the outlaws were killed save for one: Clay McFord. Not a single lawman was struck.

Holcomb approached McFord, who had two bullet wounds in one leg. Placing the point of his revolver against the outlaw's head, the sheriff asked him where the bank loot was. McFord just laughed, telling the sheriff that they had hidden the gold and that if he was killed no one would ever find it. McFord was tied to a horse, transported back to Saratoga, and placed in the town jail to await trial for bank robbery and murder. While the posse was in pursuit of the robbers, bank teller Childers died from his wound.

McFord was tried on August 3, and a six-man jury found

him guilty of both charges. The presiding judge, Zachary Scott, sentenced McFord to die by hanging. After the trial, Holcomb escorted the condemned man back to his cell. During the short walk, McFord said he'd like to make a deal. He said he would trade some of the bank's money for his freedom.

After locking McFord in his cell, Holcomb went to see the banker, Knox, and informed him of the outlaw's proposition. Knox went to the jail to visit with the outlaw about the possibility of recovering the money. McFord told Knox that if he could gain his freedom, he would return half the gold the gang stole.

Knox told McFord that he was in no position to make deals, but the outlaw merely smiled and reminded the banker that only he knew where the gold was hidden. If he was hanged, he said, then no one would get it.

Holcomb and Knox adjourned to a nearby saloon to discuss McFord's offer. After nearly an hour, Holcomb convinced the banker to settle for half the money and arrange for the robber's release. During the conversation, Holcomb bargained for 10 percent of any recovered loot as a fee for taking the risk of allowing the prisoner to escape. Knox reluctantly agreed.

On returning to the jail, Holcomb and Knox informed McFord that they would agree to his offer on the condition that when the transaction was completed, the outlaw would leave Wyoming for good. McFord assented and told the two men that the $68,000 in gold coins was buried at a location not far from the trail the robbers had taken out of Saratoga toward the hideout. Once he was free, he said, he would take them to the site.

Just before dawn the following morning, Sheriff Holcomb led McFord out of the jail and to a waiting saddled horse. The two men joined Knox, and together they rode out of town along the route that led to the hideout in the grove of cedar trees near the North Platte River. About halfway to the hideout, McFord reined up, pointed to a nearby outcropping of rock, and told Holcomb and Knox that the gold coins were hidden there, deep in a vertical crack near the middle of the formation.

A second later, banker Knox pulled his revolver and shot McFord twice in the chest, the force of the bullets knocking the outlaw from the horse. As McFord lay on the ground dying, he smiled at Knox and told him he had lied about where the gold was hidden just to see if the banker would keep his part of the bargain. Then the outlaw, the last man who knew the secret location of the cache, died.

Knox and Holcomb climbed to the rock outcrop and found the vertical crack McFord had described, but there was nothing inside. For the next several days, the two men returned to the area to search but were never able to find the gold.

To date, the $68,000 in stolen gold coins has never been recovered, and most believe that the fortune, worth well over $1 million today, lies not far from the trail that led from Saratoga to the cedar grove near the North Platte River.

Chapter 27

John Smith and His
Oklahoma Gold Cache

The man who lay dying on the hospital cot was only dimly aware that other people were moving about the room. He heard voices, but they sounded as if they were passing through water. He was vaguely aware that it was daytime outside; his vision and perceptions were clouded with morphine. Once, when he regained consciousness for a few moments, he thought he sensed the image of a nurse bent over him, wiping his hot face with a cool rag and murmuring soft, soothing words. The man tried to speak, but his parched throat and cracked and broken lips fought the words, keeping them trapped within. Finally, with great difficulty, he managed to weakly rasp the words, "Money," "buried," and "friends dead."

The patient, estimated to be around 35 years old, wandered in and out of consciousness for the next two weeks, his only company the nurse who tended to him. Sometimes he attempted to reach out to her, and occasionally he tried to speak. Following these feeble efforts, he lapsed back into unconsciousness.

Though the patient seldom remained lucid for more than a few minutes at a time, he seemed to be aware that he was dying. From several places on his body he felt the pain and itch of the numerous wounds he had received days earlier. By the time the surgeon had examined, cleaned, and bandaged the wounds, he had removed a total of seven bullets. Many of the projectiles had reached vital organs and the loss of blood had been critical. As the unconscious man was carried from the operating table to a cot in a corner room of the tiny hospital, the doctor told the attending nurses that he did not believe the man would live through the night.

Miraculously, the patient, who possessed no identification, clung tenaciously to life for several more days. From time to time he would thrash about on the cot, screaming, his eyes wide with fear. Once, when the nurse visited him to change his bandages, she thought she saw tears in his eyes.

One day, as the nurse spoon-fed the dying man some broth, he rose clumsily to a seated position and looked around, confused. As the nurse helped him lie back down and placed a pillow behind his head, he reached out and gently took her hand, begging her to sit with him a while. For nearly an hour the woman remained, not a word spoken between them. Finally, the stranger looked up at the nurse and asked for permission to explain how he came to be in the hospital and how he had acquired his wounds. As she listened patiently, the dying man unfolded the incredible story of a bank robbery, a frightening escape across the Oklahoma prairie, a deadly fight with Indians, the death of his two companions, and the hasty burial of a fortune in gold and silver coins.

Two months earlier, the dying man, who referred to himself only as John Smith, was returning from the buffalo range with two companions he called Kelley and Morton. Having made their living as hide hunters for years, the three longtime friends had grown disappointed with the dwindling herds of the great shaggy animals and decided that it was time to find some other line of work. The problem was that none of them had ever done much of anything except for hunting and skinning buffalo.

One evening, while seated around a campfire somewhere on the broad, yellow prairie of western Kansas, one of the men suggested that they rob a bank. After discussing their bad luck and discovering that they had less than five dollars between them and no chance of finding work, the notion of robbing a bank took on significance.

Arriving in the bustling town of Wichita several days later, the three men set up camp a half-mile away. For the next three days, they rode into town to observe the comings and goings of bank employees and customers. Finally, they decided to rob the bank when it opened on the morning of the fourth day.

At precisely 9:00 a.m., the owner of the bank was unlocking the front door when Smith walked up and shoved the barrel of his revolver into his back and hastened him inside. Kelly followed while Morton stood guard outside. Within a matter of minutes, several canvas bags were filled with gold and silver coins from the bank's safe. This done, the owner was tied, gagged, and shoved to the floor behind his desk. Carrying the heavy sacks, the three bandits ran out of the bank to their horses, mounted, and fled the town.

For the next two days, they traveled in a southerly direction, riding hard and stopping only to let their horses water and graze. Smith, Kelley, and Morton subsisted only on hard biscuits made in camp days earlier. Their horses, unaccustomed to the added weight of the heavy sacks of coins, occasionally faltered and stumbled. After the third day of hard riding, the three outlaws crossed the state line into Indian Territory (today Oklahoma). When they were certain they were not being followed, they stopped in a grove of elm trees beside the trail and set up camp.

Around the campfire that night, the three friends counted the money they had taken from the bank and were surprised to discover that they had escaped with nearly $50,000 in gold and silver coins. They decided to travel on to Texas and use the money to set themselves up with a fine ranch.

For the next several days, the outlaws continued on an erratic, southerly course toward Texas. One afternoon, while riding across an open prairie, Morton's horse began to have difficulty walking. The men feared that if the animal could not continue, Morton would be forced to walk and his share of the loot would have to be divided and carried by the two other already-overburdened horses.

As the travelers passed through a region near present-day Caddo County, Kelley recalled a time several years earlier when he had traveled through the nearby Wichita Mountains. There, he told his friends, they would be able to find fresh water, shelter, and wild game while men and horses rested from the tiresome journey. They headed in that direction.

Their stay in the Wichita Mountains, however, was not as peaceful as they had hoped. From the day the three men arrived, they spotted Comanche Indians watching them from nearby ridges and hilltops. Kelley informed his companions that Comanches were regarded as the most bloodthirsty residents of the Great Plains. Camp that night was subdued and quiet, and none of the men got much sleep. After their third day in the Wichita Mountains, the three outlaws packed up and continued their journey. Though the lame horse struggled with its load, it was able to walk at a cautious pace.

Late one afternoon, the men stopped at a spring. As men and horses watered, Morton spotted 40 mounted and armed warriors two miles back on the trail they were traveling. The Indians were advancing rapidly. The outlaws mounted up quickly and spurred their horses southward. As soon as the Comanches spotted the fleeing riders, they charged toward them, yelling and brandishing lances, rifles, and bows and arrows.

After riding only a few hundred yards, it became obvious to the outlaws that their heavily-laden mounts would never outdistance the Indians' swift, plains-bred ponies. Morton suggested that they cut the sacks of money loose to lighten their loads, but Smith and Kelley resisted the idea.

Suddenly, Morton's crippled horse stopped altogether and collapsed to the ground. Smith and Kelly reined up, dismounted, and, along with Morton, took shelter behind the fallen animal. As the lame horse kicked furiously and tried to rise, Kelley shot it through the head. Seconds later, the Comanches halted less than 100 yards away and began firing arrows and bullets at the three men hunkered behind the dead animal. For an hour, the outlaws kept their heads down, cowering behind their accidental and insufficient shelter. Morton, believing a show of courage and firepower would discourage the Indians, rose up and took aim at a cluster of Indian riders. He was immediately struck in the abdomen by a bullet. Bleeding profusely, he dropped to the ground, howling in pain.

For the next several hours, the Indians lofted arrows in a high, wide parabola toward their enemy and fired away at the dead horse with their rifles. Blood from the dead animal splattered onto the defenders, and the horse soon resembled a pincushion, with at least 100 arrows piercing its hide. The warriors with guns took up positions around the three outlaws in attempts to get clean shots at them, but fortunately for the defenders, they had sufficient ammunition to keep the Comanches at a respectable distance.

At sunset, Morton died from his wound. As Smith and Kelley lay in terrified silence next to their dead companion, the Comanches retreated a mile and a half northward back up the trail, where they set up camp for the night. When it grew dark, Smith and Kelley could see their campfires in the distance and presumed the Indians had abandoned the fight until morning. Using their hands and belt knives, the two men excavated a shallow hole and buried Morton.

For several more hours, the two men sat in the dark, considering their options, when Kelly suggested that they make a run for it. While Smith kept watch on the Indian camp, Kelley went in search of their horses. Within minutes, he found them grazing a short distance away, still saddled and still burdened with the bank robbery loot. When Kelley returned with the mounts, the two men removed Morton's share of the heist and distributed it between the two remaining steeds. Once the horses were loaded, the two men mounted and slipped away to the south.

Just as they abandoned the barely-significant protection afforded by Morton's dead horse, a hint of dawn appeared on the eastern horizon, barely illuminating the stark prairie.

The two men had covered little more than a mile when they heard the screams of the Indians in pursuit. Lashing and spurring their horses, each one now encumbered with more weight than before, the two outlaws tried to coax the animals to greater speeds.

It was not to happen. Within minutes, the Comanches were almost upon them. Kelley spotted a buffalo wallow near the trail and led Smith toward it. With hardly any protection at all, they dismounted and took up positions flat on their bellies, just below the rim of the depression, and fired into the attacking line of Indians, killing several. In the process, both Smith and Kelly received several wounds from Comanche bullets and arrows.

For the rest of the day, the Indians launched several frontal attacks, only to be repelled by the bullets of their quarry. Around noon, Kelley was killed when a bullet slammed into his face. Though he had lost a great deal of blood from his wounds, Smith was able to maintain his defensive position until sundown, at which time the Indians once again retreated some distance away and set up camp. For the second night in a row, Smith buried a friend. Into a shallow hole he painfully excavated, he placed Kelley's body, along with his saddle, two revolvers, and rifle.

After refilling the crude grave, John noticed the two horses grazing nearby. He retrieved them and led them to a low rise a hundred yards away, atop which grew a single tree. Here, he untied the sacks of coins and, though weakened from loss of blood, dug a second hole, into which he placed the entire robbery loot. Following this, he turned one of the horses loose, mounted the other, and continued on toward Texas. Within only a few minutes of riding away from the only tree that could be seen on this part of the prairie, he crossed what he identified as West Cache Creek, a landmark he intended to use when he returned to dig up the fortune in coins.

Days later, he forded the Red River, entered Texas, and rode on to Dallas. He was found lying in the middle of the town's main street early one morning, with blood from his reopened wounds seeping into the dirt. His horse was nowhere to be found.

When John Smith finished relating his tale to the nurse, he sighed and told her he realized he would never be able to return for the money. He asked her to find it and return it to the bank in Wichita, Kansas. Before falling asleep, Smith thanked the nurse for her kindness. Two days later, he was dead.

Five more years passed before the nurse resigned from her position at the hospital. She immediately organized an expedition party and set forth into Indian Territory in an attempt to locate Smith's buried fortune. Following the directions she had gleaned from Smith's descriptions of the region, she concentrated her search in an area approximately four miles west-southwest of the present-day town of Geronimo, near the line that separated Comanche and Cotton Counties. The landscape she encountered in this region closely matched the descriptions provided by Smith. On arriving in this area, her party was constantly harassed by Indians and she soon abandoned the search.

More years passed, and Indian Territory was eventually opened up for settlement. Believing it was now safe to travel into this part of Oklahoma, the nurse organized a second expedition to try and locate the treasure. This time, she found what she believed was the actual site where the three bank robbers had defended themselves against the Comanches while taking shelter behind the dead horse, but from that point she was unable to interpret the rest of Smith's directions. Frustrated at every turn, she finally decided to abandon the search and return to Dallas.

For years, only a handful of people were aware of the story of John Smith's flight from the Comanches and the subsequent caching of the robbery loot somewhere on the prairie. Those who did were intrigued by an article that appeared in the October 18, 1907, issue of the Lawton, Oklahoma, Daily News–Republican. Under the headline "Human Form Unearthed in Big Pasture," the article related how two Cotton County farmers had found the muzzle of a rifle sticking out of the ground and decided to investigate. After digging just a few inches into the soil, they found, in addition to the rifle, a human skeleton, two revolvers, and a saddle. The saddle was described as being in fairly good condition, and when it was cleaned, the name A. E. Kelley was seen branded onto the skirts.

To those who were aware of the significance of this find, it meant that the treasure was buried nearby, on a low rise upon which grew a solitary tree. Unfortunately, the two farmers refused to reveal the location of their find, saying only that it was near an old buffalo wallow not far from West Cache Creek.

In 1910, another startling discovery was made. Less than three miles north of the site where Kelley's remains were found, a second skeleton was discovered where runoff from a severe rainstorm had eroded a shallow incision into the surface of the prairie. This skeleton was found at the exact location where the nurse believed the three outlaws had defended themselves against the attacking Comanches. The remains were undoubtedly Morton's.

To date, there is no evidence that the nearly $50,000 in gold and silver coins buried on the Oklahoma plains near West Cache Creek has ever been discovered. The unclaimed cache is now worth several times its original value.

Chapter 28

Matt Borden and the Hallelujah Gulch Robbery Loot

Though never as famous as the Hole in the Wall Gang, Wyoming's Hallelujah Gulch Gang nevertheless struck terror into the hearts of Sweetwater County residents. Between the 1860s and 1880s, stagecoach robbers had become almost commonplace in Sweetwater County, and a number of outlaw gangs were responsible. The most successful of these gangs was led by a tough named Matt Borden. Borden, along with six to seven armed and experienced robbers, preyed on Huddleston-Downing stagecoaches, and most of the robberies took place at a location known as the Narrows, near Green River.

After robbing a stagecoach of its strongbox and mail bag, Borden and his Hallelujah Gulch Gang would turn to the passengers and relieve them of watches, jewelry and money, and

intended to rob a few more stagecoaches, divide up the money, and leave the area for good. Borden told the doctor that all of his companions had been killed and that as soon as he was able to travel, he would return to the gulch and dig up the money and gold for himself. He would be rich, he said, and would travel to California, where he planned to live like a king.

The doctor gave Borden the bad news. He told the outlaw that he didn't expect him to live more than a few hours, that he had lost too much blood. The diagnosis angered Borden and he threatened to shoot the physician. When the reality of his situation finally sank in, however, Borden broke down and cried, ruing the day he went astray and fell in with bad men.

An hour later, Borden called the doctor into his room. He thanked him for his efforts to save his life and said that he wanted to tell him the location of the buried fortune in Hallelujah Gulch. He said the hiding place was so simple that it would be the first place a search party would overlook. Borden asked the doctor for a pencil and a piece of paper so he could draw a map. The doctor went to fetch the requested items, but when he returned, Borden said that he was tired and wanted to sleep for a while. When the doctor looked in on him an hour later, he was dead. He had written nothing on the piece of paper.

At the first opportunity the doctor informed the sheriff about his patient and told him what the outlaw had said about the robbery loot buried in Hallelujah Gulch. He related what Borden said about the treasure's being cached in an obvious place.

The sheriff passed this information along to officials at the stage line, and together the two agencies organized a group of men to search the canyon in hope of finding the loot and returning it to the stagecoach company. Though they searched for days, they found nothing.

During the 1930s, an aged hermit took up residence in the outlaw cabin in Hallelujah Gulch. From time to time, the old man traveled to Green River, where he worked odd jobs for a few days to make some money to buy food, then returned to the canyon.

During his stay in the cabin, the hermit was plagued by packrats, so he decided to try to find their nest and rid the place of them. He found a small opening in the rocks of one wall where the rodents came and went. He followed a narrow rodent trail from the cabin to a location several yards away and, after moving some rocks and branches, found the nest.

The hermit pulled apart the nest, and as he did, he spotted the edge of a leather pouch that appeared to have been buried in the ground. He lifted the pouch, opened it, and poured out sixteen $20 gold pieces

The following day, the hermit took his newfound wealth to Green River and began ordering drinks at a tavern. After five or six drinks, he became quite inebriated and began bragging about his discovery of gold coins in the packrats' nest. He did not, however, reveal that the location was in Hallelujah Gulch. Several hours later, when the old man staggered out of the bar, he stepped into the street in front of a pair of speeding horses pulling a wagon. He was knocked to the ground and badly injured.

Patrons of the tavern carried the hermit to the doctor's house and explained what had happened. The old man had several broken bones, a punctured lung, and he was bleeding internally. The physician promised that he would do what he could, but moments later, the old man died. He never revealed the source of his coins.

Because no one ever associated the old hermit with Hallelujah Gulch until many years later, there was no effort to travel to the canyon to search for the old cabin and the cache. Furthermore, at the time, many residents of Green River believed that the outlaws were still hiding out there.

Years later, when the outlaw gangs had been driven from the area, men occasionally entered Hallelujah Gulch in hope of finding the buried robbery loot. Though many encountered the old cabin deep in the canyon, no one has been able to find the cache.

The remains of the cabin can still be seen today. The roof has long since caved in and the walls have mostly tumbled down. Thick brush has grown up around the site, and a visitor must be wary of the rattlesnakes that dine on the canyon's packrats.

In an unknown location a short distance behind the ruins lie the spoils of several stagecoach robberies. Researchers estimate the value of the cache to be worth at least $1 million.

Chapter 29

The Newton Brothers' Lost Train Robbery Gold

Most people associate train robberies with the outlaw west, but the truth is that hundreds such holdups have occurred in almost every one of the United States. One man, virtually unknown to Americans at large, robbed more trains and accumulated more money from his activities than Jesse James, Butch Cassidy, and the Dalton Gang put together. His name was Willis Newton, he was from Uvalde, Texas, and he planned and, with the help of his three brothers, executed the greatest train robbery in American history. It took place on June 12, 1924, near Rondout, Illinois, a railroad junction located 30 miles north of Chicago, Illinois. Close to $3 million worth of currency and bonds that were being shipped from the Federal Reserve Bank of Chicago to banks in the Northeast were taken.

Like a number of train robbers, the Newton brothers were raised in a Texas farm family. Not content to labor in the cotton fields all day, the brothers – Willis, Joe, Jess, and Doc – were eager for other opportunities. Between 1914 and 1924, the gang robbed trains and banks. Joe estimated that over the years, the brothers stole close to $6 million.

Willis was the first of the brothers to engage in crime, and the others followed a short time later. In 1909, he and Doc were arrested for stealing cotton and for vagrancy and were sentenced to two years each in a Texas penitentiary. Both escaped but were recaptured and sentenced to serve more time. Texas governor O. B. Colquitt later pardoned both of the young men.

Prison provided no lessons at all for Willis, other than causing him to become more determined than before to engage in crime. Thus far, his entire life had been little more than poverty and backbreaking farm labor. He also maintained that he had been wrongly charged in many instances and unjustly imprisoned. When he was released from confinement, he was, according to one writer, determined to "become the outlaw that the authorities envisioned him to be."

Following his first train robbery in 1914, Willis found other outlets for his penchant for stealing. In 1917, he was arrested on a charge of bank robbery in Marble Falls, Texas, but released a short time later. Without allowing much time to pass, Willis turned to petty theft and gambling. He was arrested again and sent to the penitentiary but served less than a year when he was pardoned once again, this time by Governor William P. Hobby.

Gathering about him a small gang at this time (not his brothers), Willis robbed stores in Mineral Wells, Denton, and Abilene, Texas. They stole money, clothing, tools, and shoes.

In Winters, Texas, he and his team stole $3,500 worth of Liberty Bonds from a bank. During pursuit by law enforcement authorities, one of the gang members was shot and killed. Wasting no time at all, the gang went on to rob banks and stores in Texas, Oklahoma, Kansas, and Michigan.

In 1920, brother Joe joined Willis and, along with a man named Brentwood Glasscock, robbed banks in Nebraska and Iowa. (At least one writer gives his name as Joe Glasscock). Joe Newton was only 19 years old at the time. In 1921, Willis talked brothers Doc and Jess into joining the gang. Willis was the oldest and the most experienced of the four brothers and thus assumed the mantle of leader. For the most part, the brothers concentrated on robbing banks, but according to Joe Newton, they mixed in "an occasional train holdup for the fun of it and for the booty that usually rode in the baggage and mail cars."

The well-established gang of four brothers, along with Glasscock and some others, went on to rob banks and trains throughout Texas, Missouri, Indiana, South Dakota, Arkansas, and in Canada. During their decade-long career as bank and train robbers, the Newton brothers appeared to be enjoying themselves at every turn. In 1976, Willis Newton was quoted as saying, "We never killed anybody and we never wanted to. All we wanted was the money . . . Robbing banks and trains was our way of getting it. That was our business."

According to Joe Newton he, along with his brothers, held up more than 80 banks. He also claimed that they robbed a total of six trains. In the process of committing all of these robberies, Joe said, they never killed anybody. It was not for lack of trying, however, for members of the gang are on record as having shot and wounded several victims.

Following years of successful train and bank robberies, the Newton brothers still longed to make a great haul – a significant heist that would set them up for years to come. They found their opportunity with a run of the Chicago, Milwaukee, and St. Paul train that carried more than $3 million for banking institutions in the east. Accompanying the Newton brothers was Brentwood Glasscock. With assistance from a postal inspector named Fahy and an elected politician named Murray, Willis Newton received the information necessary to pull the heist. Two brand-new 1924 Cadillac touring cars were stolen to assist in the getaway.

Wearing overalls and caps similar to those that the engineer and fireman wore, the brothers and their accomplices ran from a hiding place and jumped onto the blind of the car closest to the engine. From there, Willis climbed aboard the tender, made his way across the top, and dropped down into the cab of the locomotive, his revolver pointed at the engineer. At a certain point along the tracks near Rondout, the train was pulled to a halt.

The robbers made their way to the mail car. Willis tossed a container of formaldehyde through one of the car's windows, telling the messengers inside that it was poison gas. The door slid open a few seconds later. Willis ordered the mail clerks out and to lie face down on the ground. Selecting one of the clerks, Willis instructed him to toss out all of the sacks of registered mail. There were 60 of them. Other clerks were ordered to place the sacks in the two Cadillacs. This done, the robbers sped away, the robbery completely successful. But the robbers' good luck was not to last.

During the robbery, Doc had accidentally been shot by Glasscock and was bleeding badly. Willis drove straight to the hideout and instructed another accomplice to locate a doctor.

While they waited for the physician to arrive, the money from the mailbags was counted and divided. After getting his share, Jess Newton departed.

On the morning of June 14, police stormed the hideout and arrested Willis, Joe, Doc, and the elected politician. They were jailed and held for trial. Meanwhile, Jess had made his way to San Antonio spending much of his share of the loot on whiskey and women. When he was sober, he grew concerned about the large amount of robbery loot he was carrying around and decided that he needed to hide it.

One afternoon while he was in the middle of a drinking binge, Jess packed his suitcase full of his share of the money from the holdup, hailed a cab, and headed west out of San Antonio along the Old Fredericksburg Road. Jess shared his liquor with the cab driver as they rode along, and after they had traveled several miles both men were quite drunk. At one point along the road, Jess told the driver to stop. After climbing out of the cab, Jess grabbed the suitcase and walked out into the brush several yards from the road. When he was out of sight of the cab, he hid the suitcase under a large rock and staggered back to the cab and the pair returned to San Antonio. The following morning, when Jess awoke from an all-night drinking spree, he had a vague recollection of hiding the money but could not remember where. He hailed another cab and directed it back down the Old Fredericksburg Road to where he was convinced he had cached the money. Though he searched for more than an hour, he was unable to find it.

After returning to San Antonio, Jess made plans to flee to Mexico. Several days later, he was arrested and joined his brothers in jail. They were tried and sentenced to Leavenworth Prison in Kansas. Doc served six years, Willis served four, Joe served one, and Jess served nine months.

During the first few months the Newton brothers were serving their sentences, reports were issued stating that the total amount of cash, bonds, and notes stolen during the Rondout train robbery exceeded $3 million. It was also reported that while some of the money had been recovered, the majority of it was still missing. None of the Newton brothers admitted to possessing any knowledge whatsoever of the money's whereabouts.

Years later, when the Newtons were released from prison, it was presumed by law enforcement personnel that they had retrieved much of the train robbery loot from various hiding places. Jess, however, was never able to locate the cache that he placed alongside the Old Fredericksburg Road. After several fruitless searches, he finally gave up. Willis claimed that he knew where the cache was located, but when pressed, he admitted that he could never find it. As far as is known, that portion of the Rondout train robbery loot has never been found. Most researchers believe that Jess's share of the take was close to $200,000. Assuming the suitcase containing this cash was somewhat weatherproof, it may still be lying under the big rock where Jess placed it, waiting to be found.

Chapter 30

Holden Dick's
Lost Stagecoach Cache

Holden Dick was a Pit River Indian who lived in squalor on poor lands assigned to his tribe a few miles southeast of Alturas, in northern California. As an adult of 27 years, Dick's needs were simple: He required only a roof over his head and enough food to sustain him. It was all he was used to. On the few trips he made into the town of Alturas, it galled Dick to observe whites living in relative splendor on what was once the homeland of his tribe. He was determined to do something about it. Dick decided that the only way to get ahead in life was to steal from those who were better off than he.

For a time, Dick resorted to robbing lone travelers along isolated roads. Unfortunately for him, most of the travelers were nearly as poor as he, and his efforts resulted in his pocketing only a small amount of money each time. Dick was also suspected of murdering a Chinese cook and taking money from his pockets, but this was never verified. Dick decided to set his sights on richer targets.

In time, Dick learned of the transportation of gold ore from Nevada's Black Rock mining region to Sacramento, California. The route, one often used by freighters, wound through high mountain passes and across wide, low plains. On horseback, Dick scouted the region, searching for an ideal location to halt and rob one of the wagons transporting gold ore.

In mid-March of 1881, a freight wagon pulled by four stout mules carrying several hundred pounds of gold ore passed the southern edge of the Warner Mountains, near Moon Lake, on its way to Sacramento. The driver of the wagon, a veteran of dozens of trips, was accompanied by three armed guards, one in the seat beside him and two on horseback. Up ahead on the road, the driver spotted a lone rider coming toward him at a walk. As the wagon neared the rider, the driver and guards waved. The driver pulled the wagon to a halt to engage the traveler in conversation and learn something about the road conditions up ahead. The traveler, wearing a poncho pulled up to cover the lower part of his face and a wide-brimmed hat pulled low over his eyes, reined up. A second later, he yanked a rifle from beneath the poncho and shot and killed the two mounted guards. The driver and the guard seated next to him raised their hands in surrender.

Holden Dick ordered the driver and surviving guard to drop their weapons, climb down from the wagon, and begin walking toward the nearest settlement, some 20 miles to the south. Once the two men were out of sight around a bend in the road, Dick tied his horse to the tailgate of the wagon, climbed into the driver's seat, and whipped the mules to a fast pace and steered them to the north. With a calmness belying his violent crime, Dick headed toward a predetermined location in a remote canyon on the western slope of the southern part of the Warner Mountains. There, he intended to cache the gold in a cave. Holden Dick, a normally reclusive Pit River Indian who wore rags for clothes, had come into possession of a fortune in gold ore.

On driving the freight wagon deep into the canyon, Dick cached the gold in a shallow shelter cave. This done, he constructed a crude rock wall across a portion of the cave entrance. Here he lived throughout most of the year, venturing back to his family's homesite from time to time for visits. He told no one about his fortune in gold. When necessary, he traveled to Alturas or Susanville to purchase supplies and provisions. While in one or the other of these towns, he would idle away evenings in taverns, always paying for his drinks with gold nuggets. Because he normally carried only small amounts of the ore at time, most people believed that Dick was working a poor mining claim somewhere back up in the mountains.

Contrary to his normal habit of transporting small amounts of gold, Dick arrived at a Susanville tavern one day carrying an unusually heavy pack, from which he pulled a handful of gold nuggets to pay for his drinks. Several men playing cards at a nearby table spotted the gleaming gold and invited the Indian to join them. Politely, Dick refused but purchased a round of drinks for the group. He was lured into conversation with them and, while fielding questions from the card players, admitted that his pack was filled with gold ore. When they asked where it had come from, Dick remained silent. The following day, Dick loaded some recently purchased supplies onto his spare horse and rode back toward the Warner Mountains.

Dick reached the southern limit of the Madeline Plains around noon, when he chanced to look back along the trail and saw that he was being followed. Even though the trackers were a half-mile away, he recognized two of them as the card players who had questioned him about his gold. That evening, Dick stopped to set up camp for the night, built a fire, and laid out his bedroll, all within sight of the men following him, who watched from a ravine 200 yards away. When the trackers were certain that the Indian had bedded down for the night, they retreated farther back down the road and set up their own camp. Two hours later, as Dick's fire burned down to coals, he silently and efficiently loaded his gear and rode away.

Dick was followed on several other occasions while returning to his cave in the Warner Mountains from Susanville. Once, a party of four trackers trailed him to the very mouth of the canyon in which his secret cache was located. Dick hid behind some rocks and waited with his rifle. When the trackers came in sight, he fired at one of them, a man named Samuel B. Shaw. Shaw was killed instantly, and the remaining tracker fled.

In March 1885, Dick rode into Susanville and was approached by Sheriff C. C. Rachford who arrested him for Shaw's murder. Dick was placed in the Susanville jail to await trail. Two months later, the trial was held and Dick was found guilty. The judge sentenced him to be "hanged by the neck until dead." Appeals were filed, and it was nearly 10 months later when a new trial date was finally set.

On the evening of January 23, 1886, Holden Dick was sitting in his jail cell, contemplating his chances in the upcoming trail. (One account states that the date was January 28). In the cell next to him was a man named Vicente Olivas, who had been convicted of murdering a man named Griffith Logan near Pittville, California, and who was awaiting sentencing. Late that night, a group of four men intent on learning where Dick had hidden his gold gained access to his cell. They offered to free him if he would agree to lead them to the gold. Dick refused, stating that he would rather hang than reveal the location of his gold cache to white men.

Enraged, the quartet unlocked Dick's cell and dragged the Indian out into the street. For reasons unclear, they also removed Olivas from his cell and pushed him outside to stand with Dick. In the darkness of the overcast night, the four men threatened to kill the Indian unless he told them where the gold was hidden. Dick continued to refuse and at one point spit into the face of one of his captors. Enraged, the man beat Dick mercilessly. For the next hour, Dick was interrogated, whipped, and tortured. Finally, he died at the hands of the men who would have his fortune. Turning their frustration toward Olivas, they likewise beat him until he was near death.

Frustrated and angry, the gang dragged Dick's body, along with that of Olivas, into a nearby blacksmith shop and hanged both of them from ropes tied to a rafter. At first, Dick was hung by his long hair, his scalp nearly ripped from his head. His body was covered in blood. The only man who could have led the four greedy men to the rich cache of gold ore was dead.

Few today outside of northern California are aware of the story of Holden Dick's lost gold cache – a fortune stashed in a shallow cave somewhere in the Warner Mountains. It is believed that the canyon in which the cave is located is one that extends from Eagle Peak, a prominent landmark in the southern part of the range. Occasionally, treasure hunters arrive in the area in search of Dick's gold cache, but to date, its discovery has not been reported.

Boessenecker, John. Bandido: The Life and Times of Tiburcio Vasquez. Norman: University of Oklahoma Press. 2010.

Chamberlain, Kathleen. Victorio: Apache Warrior and Chief. Norman: University of Oklahoma Press. 2007.

Dalton, Emmett, and Jack Jungmeyer. When the Daltons Rode. Garden City, New York: Doubleday, Doran, and Company. 1931.

Farmer, Randolph W. Curly Bill: Horsethief, Cattle Dealer, Murderer, Lawman; 1858–1909. Tucson, Arizona: Westernlore Press. 2012.

Gatto, Steve. The Real Wyatt Earp: A Documentary Biography. Silver City, New Mexico: High Lonesome Books. 2000.

Green, Carl R., and William R. Sanford. The Dalton Gang. Berkeley Heights, New Jersey: Enslow Publisher. 1995.

Jameson, W. C. Lost Mines and Buried Treasures of Arkansas. Nashville, Tennessee: Goldminds Publishing, LLC. 2011.

_____. Lost Mines and Buried Treasures of Old Wyoming. Glendo, Wyoming: High Plains Press. 2010.

_____. Lost Treasures of American History. Boulder, Colorado: Taylor Trade Publishing. 2006.

_____. Buried Treasures of the Great Plains. Little Rock, Arkansas: August House Publishers, Inc. 1998.

_____. Buried Treasures of California. Little Rock, Arkansas: August House Publishers, Inc. 1995.

_____. Buried Treasures of the Pacific Northwest. Little Rock, Arkansas: August House Publishers, Inc. 1995.

_____. Buried Treasures of the Rocky Mountain West. Little Rock, Arkansas: August House Publishers, Inc. 1993.

_____. Buried Treasures of the South. Little Rock, Arkansas: August House Publishers, Inc. 1992.

_____. Buried Treasures of Texas. Little Rock, Arkansas: August House Publishers, Inc. 1991.

Latta, Frank F. Dalton Gang Days. Santa Cruz, California: Bear State Books. 1976.

Preece, Harold. The Dalton Gang: End of an Outlaw Era. Winter Park, Florida: Hastings House Publishers, Inc. 1963.

Thrapp, Dan L. Encyclopedia of Frontier Biography. Spokane, Washington: The Arthur H. Clarke Co. 1990.

_____. Victorio and the Mimbres Apaches. Norman: University of Oklahoma Press. 1974.

About the Author

W. C. Jameson is the award-winning author of over 100 books. He has served as a consultant for film and appears regularly on television as an analyst and narrator. He has contributed music to the soundtracks of seven films, has recorded 10 albums of original songs, and has been the subject of two documentaries. When not locked away in his writing studio working on books, he travels the country performing his songs at music festivals, colleges and universities, concert halls, roadhouses, and on television. He lives in Llano, Texas.